BOOK SENSE
BEST
CHILDREN'S
BOOKS

Also by Book Sense

BOOK SENSE BEST BOOKS: *125 Favorite Books Recommended by Independent Booksellers*

BOOK SENSE
BEST
CHILDREN'S
BOOKS

240 Favorites

for All Ages

Recommended by

Independent Booksellers

Compiled by Book Sense

Edited by Mark Nichols

Foreword by Cornelia Funke

NEWMARKET PRESS • NEW YORK

This book is published in the United States of America.

First Edition

ISBN 1-55704-679-4

10 9 8 7 6 5 4 3 2 1

Library of Congress Cataloging-in-Publication Data

Book Sense best children's books : favorites for all ages recommended by independent booksellers / foreword by Cornelia Funke ; compiled by Book Sense ; edited by Mark Nichols.
    p. cm.
  Includes index.
  ISBN 1-55704-679-4 (cloth : alk. paper)
  1. Children—Books and reading—United States—Bibliography. 2. Children's literature—Bibliography. 3. Best books—United States. I. Nichols, Mark II. Book Sense (Program)
  Z1037.B7219 2005
  011.62—dc22
                         2005024102

QUANTITY PURCHASES
Companies, professional groups, clubs, and other organizations may qualify for special terms when ordering quantities of this title. For information or to request a complete catalog, write Special Sales Department, NEWMARKET PRESS, 18 EAST 48TH STREET, NEW YORK, NY 10017; call (212) 832-3575; FAX (212) 832-3629; or e-mail info@newmarketpress.com.

www.newmarketpress.com

Designed by Kevin McGuinness

Manufactured in the United States of America.

CONTENTS

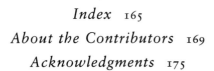

❧ LIST OF ILLUSTRATIONS

Foreword

CORNELIA FUNKE

WHEN BOOK-O-PHILES CLOSE THEIR EYES, WHAT DO THEY SEE?
A bookstore, of course, filled to the brim with books thick and thin, old and new, all of them waiting on their shelves for a hand to grab them and take them home (that is, after having paid the relatively small sum that affords such a large pleasure).

But what kind of bookstore is it?

I'd been a writer in Germany for fifteen years and visited many wonderful bookstores before I walked into my first independent bookstore in the United States. But now, when I close my eyes, I see that American store: a treasured memory of an enchanted place that could feed me for weeks with printed pages, booksellers' advice, and reading passion. A place that will surely one day find its way into one of my stories.

Back home, there are many, many independent bookstores—in fact, they are still the rule, not the exception, because in Germany the retail law allows bookstores, big or small, to sell books only at the price set by the publisher. "That sounds like paradise, Cornelia!" one priestess of American independent book passion said to me recently when I told her about this incredibly useful law. And yes, such a law does serve a valuable purpose in protecting small and independent stores, but nevertheless I found *my* book paradise here in the USA.

There are wonderful bookstores all over Europe—in Zurich, Baden-Baden, Hamburg, Salisbury, London, Venice. There are many of those magical places, built from books and booksellers' passion, where you step through a door and seem to leave everything behind (though the books within all talk about the things outside). But no, when I close my eyes, I see *your* bookstores, often hidden in small towns, sometimes in faceless malls (which may make the enchantment even more impressive), and I hear their owners telling me about the books I should read. As an author, you meet such people not only in their own stores but also at long dinners, changing seats with the arrival of each course on the menu, meeting book passion at every new table, having wonderful evenings filled with intelligent encounters—and never leaving without lists of dozens of books I couldn't wait to get my hands on. Meeting an American bookseller is a dangerous thing for a poor German with only one suitcase to fill! Where to put all the new books? I always buy too many, and I never leave one of those dangerous places empty-handed. "Bookstore," what an unassuming name! As opposed to "printed paper treasure chamber" or "book-o-phile feeding-place." No, I never leave them without piles of books...and a stupidly happy smile on my face.

Love, as we all know, is a wonderful thing, especially when the loved one feels the same. So when I fell head over heels in love with American independent bookstores, it felt like a miracle that they loved my books, too. They put them on the Book Sense list, they even gave me an important award, but best of all they gave my books to children and parents, to teachers and librarians. They gave them very special places in their stores. It is such a thrill to walk into one of them and see my books, my very own books, there on the shelves among other stories that I cherish. What a feeling, knowing that they were written in an old house in Hamburg, and traveled so far, to arrive at such a perfect home. I am sure that, if I were a book, I wouldn't wish for more (except also a space at a library, where you get hundreds of readers!).

As a thank-you, I wish I could give my independent friends the German retail law that protects the small and dedicated. Sadly, I can't. I am not even sure it will last in my home country—from time to time the European Union tries to abolish it. But I can attest to one thing: Though the German booksellers have governmental protection, it can't compare to the community the American independents have formed over the years. Their organization and enthusiasm still amazes me, and their devotion to reading is absolutely unique. Talking with American friends, I often notice that they imagine Europe to be a continent of book lovers, a paradise for literary debuts. To this I can only reply that nowhere else have I met so much book passion as in America. I sometimes wish that, instead of piles of books, I could pack some of the independent booksellers that I've met into my bags and bring them back to Germany so that they could spread their words of passion in the hearts of the children, parents, teachers, and librarians over there.

Wouldn't that be a good last sentence?

But…

(Yes, I know, there is a "but.")

But independent booksellers, to whom this preface is a love letter, are an endangered species, like so many other wonderful creatures on our planet. They work too hard and they don't earn half as much as they deserve for those precious words they spread; for the irreplaceable work they do for their communities; for the pleasure they bring to children and their parents. The result all too often is that their own children decide not to continue the work that kept their mothers and fathers away from home for so long. Many independent bookstores then vanish. One enchanted book island after another sinks into the ocean of indifference. And the only thing I can do about it, as a writer, is to keep on writing. Writing, and hoping that my books sell enough to keep some of those treasure islands afloat, buoyed up by paper, ink, and words, words, words....

Introduction

MARK NICHOLS
BOOK SENSE

OVER THE PAST YEARS, CHILDREN'S BOOK PUBLISHING HAS seen an incredible increase in the number of titles produced annually. The sheer volume and variety make choosing the "right" book an evermore daunting and confusing task. This compilation of booksellers' recommendations will help guide you in your search.

Every month for general titles and three times a year for children's titles, we tally recommendations from independent booksellers. The titles that receive the strongest support from the greatest number of Book Sense booksellers make up each Book Sense Picks List. These are the books that booksellers deem most worthy of note and those they most enjoy "handselling" to their customers, based on their intimate knowledge of their customers' tastes, needs, and reading habits.

While the selections carry only a single bookseller's quote, each selection has the enthusiastic support of a chorus of booksellers, and each section is introduced by a prominent independent bookseller who offers personal and informative background about that particular reading level, as well as additional reading suggestions.

The structure of the book follows the natural growth of a child's reading skills, with sections on: Babies and Toddlers,

Picture Books for both Younger and Older Children, Chapter Books, Middle Grade, and Young Adult. These recommendations are followed by a section on Nonfiction books, organized by age level. In addition, a section on Holiday books gives children even more reason to celebrate Valentine's Day, Hanukkah, Christmas, Kwaanza, Ramadan, Chinese New Year, and more.

Special lists at the end of the book highlight favorite book series, beloved books that have been made into movies, and titles appropriate for those voracious Harry Potter fans. The variety of choices represented here offer hours of reading pleasure and challenge for all ages.

Sprinkled throughout the pages are illustrations by award-winning illustrators Jane Dyer, Ian Falconer, Brett Helquist, Betsy Lewin, Jon J Muth, David Shannon, Peter Sís, and Mark Teague. We are especially grateful to the illustrators and publishers for allowing us to publish these wonderful drawings here.

This is the second compilation we've published. *Book Sense Best Books* was published first, as part of our fifth birthday celebration in 2004. A ballot with 375 titles drawn from the top-10-ranked books on the Book Sense Picks Lists was circulated to bookseller members. More than 1,000 booksellers voted on the adult and children's titles they most enjoyed sharing with their customers. The book included The Top Picks (15 adult titles and 10 children's titles), 50 Top Reading Group Recommendations, and Top Classics for Children and Young Adults, with an appendix listing the 375 titles that were voted on.

In this second compilation from Book Sense, adults will find even more books to share with the children in their lives.

Knowledge.

Passion.

Character.

Community.

Personality.

These are the characteristics common to all independent Book Sense booksellers. They welcome your inquiries and are eager to guide you in building the best library for the child in your life. Both within these pages and at your local bookstore, experts stand ready to help you make the right choices. Happy reading!

Illustration copyright © by Jane Dyer from *Goodnight Goodnight Sleepyhead* by Ruth Krauss.
Reprinted with permission from HarperCollins Publishers.

BABIES AND TODDLERS

Dinah Paul, *A Likely Story*, Alexandria, VA

IT'S NEVER TOO EARLY TO START READING TO YOUR CHILD. In fact you can start even before the baby is born. The most important part of reading to your infant and toddler is for the child to hear your voice. They get to experience the joy of reading through you. While children may not understand the words themselves, they will experience the story through the rhythm of the words. Therefore, if you are reading a fun rhyming text like *Barnyard Dance!*, by Sandra Boynton, your child is going to hear the joy in your voice. If you are reading an action-adventure book, your infant or toddler will be hanging on the edge of his or her seat.

Illustrations are another important part of reading to your infant or toddler. Sometimes your busy toddler will not sit still for a very text-heavy book. However, if you turn the story into a game, then you will be able to hold his or her attention for longer. For example, in *Good Night, Gorilla*, by Peggy Rathmann, the only words you really have are "Good Night." However, the illustrations tell a very different story as the zookeeper locks up, while an ape unlocks doors behind him. Children will laugh out loud on the page where all you see are the eyeballs of the animals, the zookeeper, and his wife. Each time you read the story you will discover something new.

Books for infants and toddlers have the important task of being one of the first methods of teaching new ideas. However, you will find some of the most inventive learning techniques within the books for ages two and under. *Tails* and *Fuzzy Yellow Ducklings*, both by Matthew Van Fleet, teach concepts while the child sees, touches, and hears what you are talking about. In *Chicka Chicka Boom Boom,* by Bill Martin Jr. and John Archambault, children not only learn the alphabet, they see upper- and lower-case letters and a fun rhyme to help them remember their ABCs.

The most important part about reading with your infant and toddler is to have fun! Pick books that you enjoy and your child will follow your lead.

THE ALPHABET ROOM
 BY SARA PINTO

"A unique and lavish feast for the eyes. This fancy board book brings the alphabet alive with interactive flaps and something new to look at each time the book is opened."
—Sarah Parker, *Scott's Bookstore*, Mount Vernon, WA

BACKPACK BABY
 BY MIRIAM COHEN

"I love the scenes of baby and his daddy experiencing the world through the baby's eyes from his perch in the backpack. A surprise ending will keep you reading this book over and over to your toddler."
—Tom Heywood, *Babbling Book*, Haines, AK

DIGGER MAN
 BY ANDREA ZIMMERMAN & DAVID CLEMESHA

"I have read a lot of construction books, but every once in a while one comes along that sets itself apart. I love *Digger Man* because it gets at every three-year-old boy's heart's desire: to be a construction worker."
—Nicole White, *Vroman's Bookstore*, Pasadena, CA

DO LIKE A DUCK DOES!
BY JUDY HINDLEY
ILLUSTRATED BY IVAN BATES

"Here's a preschool gem with tricky words that step across the page with a Sousa-like cadence, delighting children and adults alike. This is a rollicking gem of a story in itself, but with Bates' illustrations, it's irresistible!"

—**Karen Gaston**, *Butterfly Books*, DePere, WI

THE DORLING KINDERSLEY BOOK OF NURSERY RHYMES
EDITED AND ILLUSTRATED BY DEBI GLIORI

"With comforting illustrations and interesting tidbits about how the rhymes came to be, this is a very jolly, pleasing collection for every child to grow up with."

—**Carol Moyer**, *Quail Ridge Books*, Raleigh, NC

FARMER WILL
BY JANE COWEN-FLETCHER

"A little boy wants to be a farmer, so when he steps outside, he becomes Farmer Will and his stuffed animals come to life. A wonderful story to remind us of the joy and energy in a child's imagination."

—**Yvonne Kaiser**, *The Bookworm*, Omaha, NE

FIX-IT
BY DAVID McPHAIL

"When the TV won't work, Emma demands it be fixed. Cranky young Emma has to be entertained while waiting, first with a balloon, then with a song, and finally with a book. By the time Papa discovers that the TV is unplugged, Emma is too deep into the book to care about the TV anymore!"
— Linda Hillegass, *Lee Booksellers*, Lincoln, NE

GOODNIGHT GOODNIGHT SLEEPYHEAD
BY RUTH KRAUSS
ILLUSTRATED BY JANE DYER

"This is a beautiful, newly illustrated edition of an old favorite. Warm fuzzies reach out from the pages as you work your way to sleepy time. A true delight!"
— Lois Proctor, *The Bookseller*, Ardmore, OK

HOW TO CATCH A STAR
BY OLIVER JEFFERS

"A must-have children's book. This is a charming story of a little boy who wants to befriend a star and his quest in doing so. It's the perfect tale for anyone who has ever chased a dream and has not given up. With beautiful illustrations, this is a great gift for all."
— Michelle Jammes, *Inkwood Books*, Tampa, FL

HUG

BY JEZ ALBOROUGH

"A child need only look at the pictures and learn the word 'hug' to delight over and over in the illustrations and the love in this book. A new favorite!"

—Carolyn Chesser, *Bayou Book Co.*, Niceville, FL

I LOVE MY LITTLE STORYBOOK

BY ANITA JERAM

"You know a book that makes you laugh out loud is a winner. A sweet, but never saccharine, story celebrating the joy and magic of reading and books, and Jeram's trademark adorable bunnies are the cutest fairies ever to inhabit a picture book!"

—Kathleen Carey, *The Little Book House of Stuyvesant Plaza*, Albany, NY

KISS GOOD NIGHT

BY AMY HEST
ILLUSTRATED BY ANITA JERAM

"This is a sweet children's story about a little bear who isn't ready to go to sleep until Mrs. Bear gives him many goodnight kisses! Anita Jeram is the illustrator of everyone's favorite, *Guess How Much I Love You*. I predict this will turn into a favorite bedtime story for preschoolers."

—Mary-Ann Frischkorn, *The Learned Owl Book Shop*, Hudson, OH

KNICK-KNACK PADDYWHACK

BY PAUL O. ZELINSKY

"Zelinsky has created a masterpiece of moving parts to the well-known children's song. With every reading, you see new things and understand more of this brilliant author's sense of humor and knowledge."

—Lisa Schmitt, *Wild Rumpus*, Minneapolis, MN

LITTLE HOUSE, LITTLE TOWN
BY SCOTT BECK

"In simple but lovely writing—peaceful and rhythmic—this book follows a day in the life of a young family as they go to their favorite places all around the town. *Little House, Little Town* invites both adults and children to quiet their busy lives and yet still take an interesting exploration of the world around them."

—**Hilary Taber**, *Vroman's Bookstore*, Pasadena, CA

MAMA HEN AND HER BABY CHICKS 1, 2, 3
BY ALISON MORRIS AND BECK WARD
ILLUSTRATED BY SAMI SWEETEN

"This delightful four-in-one interactive board book in the shape of a hen 'lays' three story eggs that tell about the early adventures of Mama Hen's little chicks. Playful illustrations and simple stories make this a great book for infants and toddlers."

—**Sandy Johnson**, *The Galaxy Bookshop*, Hardwick, VT

MUNG-MUNG
A FOLD-OUT BOOK OF ANIMAL SOUNDS
BY LINDA SUE PARK
ILLUSTRATED BY DIANE BIGDA

"This Newbery winner has created a fold-out guessing-game book that provides a unique approach to animal sounds in different languages. Which animal says 'ga-ga' in Japanese, but 'quack-quack' in English?"
—Nancy Lankton, *Moloney's Books*, Marion, OH

THE OWL WHO WAS AFRAID OF THE DARK
BY JILL TOMLINSON
ILLUSTRATED BY PAUL HOWARD

"A young barn owl does not like the dark, but meets several people who help him discover the night's wonder. Howard's soft, lush illustrations are comforting, and parents and children alike will enjoy this reissue of a classic 1968 book."
—Tami Edwards, *The Children's Corner Bookshop*,
Spokane, WA

PETIT CONNOISSEUR: ART
BY KAREN SALMANSOHN
ILLUSTRATED BY BRIAN STAUFFER

"Finally a coffee-table board book for babies and their ultra-cool adult companions! This witty little book is a work of art with a funky collage and a super-hip sensibility."

—**Dana Harper**, *Brystone Children's Books*, Fort Worth, TX

TAILS
BY MATTHEW VAN FLEET

"*Tails* is an interactive book of extraordinary grandeur. You will pull, lift, touch, and smell your way through this delightful journey, while learning to identify numerous animals as you count them from one to ten."

—**Liz Sandler**, *Wild Rumpus*, Minneapolis, MN

TEN LITTLE FISH
BY AUDREY WOOD
ILLUSTRATED BY BRUCE WOOD

"In this counting book for the twenty-first century, the brilliant Audrey Wood takes us on a journey through the sea with computer illustrations provided by her talented son. Any fan of *Finding Nemo* will surely be thrilled with this fun adventure."

—**Erin Shuster**, *Schuler Books & Music*, Lansing, MI

WILL YOU CARRY ME?

BY HELEEN VAN ROSSUM
ILLUSTRATED BY PETER VAN HARMELEN

"Thomas is tired after a long morning playing in the park and wants his mother to carry him home. But this creative mom has lots of tricks up her sleeve to keep her boy moving. This is an energetic tale, illustrated with verve, and one preschoolers will want to hear over and over."
—Marge Grutzmacher, *Passtimes Books*, Sister Bay, WI

WOOLEYCAT'S MUSICAL THEATER
(BOOK WITH AUDIO CD)

BY DENNIS HYSOM
ILLUSTRATED BY CHRISTINE WALKER

"The text and lyrics consist of cleverly fractured Mother Goose rhymes that add up to a ten-song musical. The illustrations are adorable, and the musical accompaniment is sprightly and beautifully produced."
—Lilla Weinberger, *Readers' Books*, Sonoma, CA

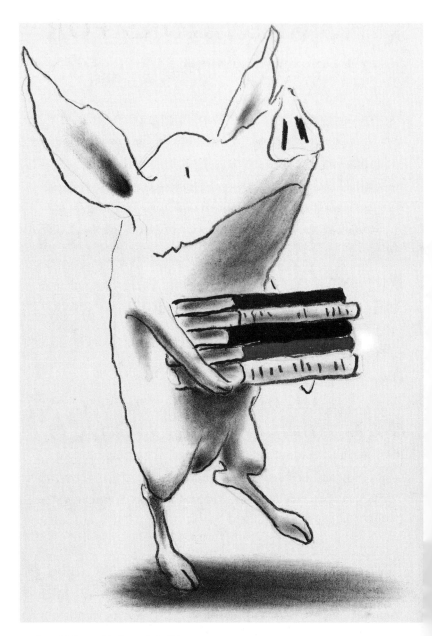

From *Olivia*, copyright © 2000 by Ian Falconer

PICTURE BOOKS FOR YOUNGER CHILDREN

Valerie Koehler, *Blue Willow Bookshop*, Houston, TX

OH, THE JOYS OF SNUGGLING UP IN A BIG EASY CHAIR WITH at least one precious child sharing each page of a picture book! When the illustrations and words come together in perfect harmony, the story will live in your collective memories for years to come. How many times have you looked for the mouse in the pages of *Goodnight Moon*? Have you laughed at the antics of a girl named *Eloise* living in a very special hotel? Were you moved to tears upon sharing the story of a young child in a forest at night, listening for a great owl in *Owl Moon*?

Picture books are labors of love, a synchronicity of devoted authors and illustrators. In this day of digital distractions, a 32-page book brimming with every genre of artwork brings home both the simplicity of a bygone era and the complexity of our modern world.

When choosing a picture book to be shared, we look for certain elements. First, the text should make sense. Is there "the drama of turning the page"? Does it compel us to read the story over and over again? Like haiku, each word—each syllable—must be irreplaceable. When we read aloud, the cadence should be at once familiar and complementary to the style of the story. Second, the illustrations must not only move the story forward, but adorn it. The decisions of the illustrator should entice us to pore over all the hidden delights.

Because we have the technology to produce all manner of books today, and in prodigious quantities, it has become increasingly difficult to make wise decisions when choosing the books we want to share with our loved ones. We believe the picture books chosen by Book Sense independent booksellers represent the best of the best. These knowledgeable booksellers (who are, above all, book lovers themselves) spend hours reading new books aloud to themselves, to friends, and to family. They make painstaking decisions to stock books that will be treasured by their customers.

The books in this chapter portray the human condition as effectively as most contemporary adult literature. Many times stories open up long-deferred conversations or tackle prickly situations that we dread discussing with our children. Understand anger management with *Sometimes I'm Bombaloo*. Lighten sibling rivalries with *You're All My Favorites*. Loneliness and the pleasure of companionship are distilled beautifully in *Orville*.

You were once mesmerized by the very idea of a cow jumping over a moon; don't you recall with vivid clarity the whimsical art that proved it possible? Picture books offer solace, enlightenment, laughter, and—in a master's hands— lyrical language matched by a dreamer's graphic interpretation. We urge you to sample from this banquet of titles, to create a precious legacy for the next generation of book lovers.

AWFUL OGRE'S AWFUL DAY

BY JACK PRELUTSKY

ILLUSTRATED BY PAUL O. ZELINSKY

"I loved this book of great read-aloud poems featuring a truly awful main character, an ogre so awful that he has a skunk living in his nose! So get out your weasel grease (the really smelly kind) and prepare yourself for a funny book; a real one-of-a-kind!"

—Vincent Desjardins, *The Snow Goose Bookstore*, Stanwood, WA

THE BIG BLUE SPOT

BY PETER HOLWITZ

"This picture book has truly original art and a playful interactive storyline. A big blue spot is all alone until he meets a new friend, the reader, and a surprise friend at the end. Charming."

—Kelly Justice, *The Fountain Bookstore*, Richmond, VA

COURAGE
BY BERNARD WABER

"Add my vote to the many that this special book will receive. Waber has given us a humorous but poignant look at some very real aspects of courage in an accessible presentation. This is a book that educators, parents, and friends will be sharing for years to come. One of the best books on the subject in a long time."

—**Sheilah Egan,** *A Likely Story Children's Bookstore,*
Alexandria, VA

A DAY IN THE LIFE OF MURPHY
BY ALICE PROVENSEN

"Murphy's a hairy little terrier, a barking, shoe-chewing scamp of a dog, who provides us with an amusing day on the farm. In this appealing read-alone, or read-aloud, we see him cadging scraps in the kitchen, barely tolerating a visit to the vet, and his frenetic pre-bedtime barking session in the farmyard."

—**Jody Fickes Shapiro,** *Adventures for Kids*, Ventura, CA

Detective Larue, Letters from the Investigation, illustration copyright © 2004 by Mark Teague

DETECTIVE LARUE
LETTERS FROM THE INVESTIGATION
BY MARK TEAGUE

"Ike LaRue returns as the feisty dog who is always falsely accused...or is he? Mark Teague's fantastic illustrations give you clues leading up to the end of a mystery every kid will want to read over and over."

—**Erin Shuster**, *Schuler Books & Music*, Lansing, MI

ALSO IN THE DETECTIVE LARUE SERIES:
Dear Mrs. Larue: Letters from Obedience School

DIARY OF A WOMBAT

BY JACKIE FRENCH
ILLUSTRATED BY BRUCE WHATLEY

"Jackie French is one of my favorite discoveries. In this
hilarious picture book, she teams up with Bruce Whatley,
who perfectly illustrates a day in the life of your friendly
neighborhood wombat. Two incredible talents combine
to make this one of my favorite children's books!"
　　　—**Beth Henkes**, *University Book Store*, Bellevue, WA

DIARY OF A WORM

BY DOREEN CRONIN
ILLUSTRATED BY HARRY BLISS

"A favorite author comes up with another big family hit.
Would you believe a precocious worm who keeps a diary
documenting his life discoveries?"
　　　—**Elsie Peterson**, *The Cottage Book Shop,* Glen Arbor, MI

DON'T LET THE PIGEON DRIVE THE BUS!

BY MO WILLEMS

"Adorable pictures and a funny text make this a wonderful title for preschoolers."

—**Marty Miller**, *Copperfield Books*, Scottsbluff, NE

DON'T TAKE YOUR SNAKE FOR A STROLL

BY KARIN IRELAND

ILLUSTRATED BY DAVID CATROW

"This is an immensely readable book with exuberant illustrations. It's hard to resist the snake on a downtown stroll, frogs loose in a gourmet restaurant, and an elephant sunning itself at the beach."

—**Carol Dunn**, *Northwind Book & Fiber*, Spooner, WI

From *Duck for President*, by Doreen Cronin, illustration copyright © 2004 by Betsy Lewin

DUCK FOR PRESIDENT

⁂ BY DOREEN CRONIN
ILLUSTRATED BY BETSY LEWIN

"Candidate Duck has high aspirations in running the farm, as one thing leads to another, and soon the presidency is at hand. Complete with Cronin's version of the 'hanging chad' and a late-night saxophone appearance on television. Fun for the whole family."

—**Carl Wichman**, *Varsity Mart*, Fargo, ND

DUMPY LA RUE
BY ELIZABETH WINTHROP
ILLUSTRATED BY BETSY LEWIN

"The text and illustrations are hilarious, but best of all,
this book has a wonderful underlying message that's clear
without being preachy: Celebrate yourself and pay no
mind to the naysayers! Dumpy La Rue simply refused
to believe he couldn't dance because he was a pig."
> —**Paulette Zander**, *Happy Carrot*, Old Lyme, CT

EARTHQUACK!
BY MARGIE PALATINI
ILLUSTRATED BY BARRY MOSER

"The illustrations would be enough reason to buy this
book! Moser puts fear in the face of a chick, alarm in the
countenance of a goose, and the author takes 'The Sky is
Falling' to a new high, with a lot of clever wording and
rhyming. What an immensely fun read-aloud!"
> —**Mary Burns**, *The BookWorks*, Marysville, WA

ELENA'S SERENADE

❧ BY CAMPBELL GEESLIN
ILLUSTRATED BY ANA JUAN

"Elena, a determined young Mexican girl, has a
father who believes she is too little to practice his art,
and, besides, who ever heard of a girl glassblower? This
is a fun, beautiful tale about following your dreams and
a great introduction to another culture. Ana Juan's
illustrations are remarkable."

—Jill Saginario, *Wellesley Booksmith,* Wellesley, MA

FAIRY HOUSES

❧ BY TRACY KANE

"The colorful pictures and the magic of the fairies had
my daughter entranced, but what makes this a winner is
the fact that kids immediately want to go outside and build
their own fairy house. What?!? Play outside in this day and
age? Aren't we skipping the whole video game step? It was
great. We went outside, got dirty, and built the best fairy
house ever."

—Shawna Elder, *Iowa Book,* Iowa City, IA

ALSO IN THE FAIRY HOUSE SERIES:
Kristin's Fairy House, Fairy Boat, and *Fairy Flight*

A FINE, FINE SCHOOL

BY SHARON CREECH
ILLUSTRATED BY HARRY BLISS

"A proud principal thinks his school is so fine, it should
be open every day! Until Tillie visits his office and tells him
that other kinds of learning no longer occur. A delightful,
funny cautionary tale."

—**Karen Miller**, *Anderson's*, Naperville, IL

THE FROGS WORE RED SUSPENDERS

BY JACK PRELUTSKY
ILLUSTRATED BY PETRA MATHERS

"This book is one of those wonderful serendipitous
marriages of word and picture. Prelutsky's funny, light
verse begs to be read out loud, and Mather's illustrations
bring an added joy to the experience."

—**Michael Coy**, *M. Coy Books*, Seattle, WA

GASPARD AND LISA
FRIENDS FOREVER
BY ANNE GUTMAN
ILLUSTRATED BY GEORG HALLENSLEBEN

"The *Gaspard and Lisa* books are a complete delight— funny, exciting, and they teach interesting lessons. And I absolutely adore the illustrations, which are bright, cute, and certainly age-appropriate to the text. I can't say enough about them. To me, they're just perfect, some of my very favorite books."

—**Carrie Graves**, *The Happy Bookseller,* Columbia, SC

ALSO IN THE MISADVENTURES OF GASPARD AND LISA SERIES:
Gaspard and Lisa at the Museum, Gaspard on Vacation, Lisa in the Jungle, and more

GOBBLE, QUACK, MOON
BY MATTHEW GOLLUB
ILLUSTRATED BY JUDY LOVE

"Utterly fantastic. As a doting auntie, I can't wait to share it with my little niece. The music makes it even more fun. A great book for the little kid in everyone."

—**Lynn Farquhar**, *The Tattered Cover*, Denver, CO

HOW I BECAME A PIRATE

BY MELINDA LONG
ILLUSTRATED BY DAVID SHANNON

"A witty tale that pirates of all ages will enjoy. Readers will not be able to resist jumping into pirate-speak as they enjoy the catchy rhyming verse and the bold and colorful illustrations."
—**Lisa Fabiano**, *Hearts & Stars Bookshop*, Canton, MA

IN ENGLISH, OF COURSE

BY JOSEPHINE NOBISSO
ILLUSTRATED BY DASHA ZIBOROVA

"From the tale of a young Italian girl trying to get her point across to the spirited and information-filled illustrations, this delightful book is a real treat both visually and conceptually."
—**Pat Rutledge**, *A Book for All Seasons*, Leavenworth, WA

JAKE GANDER, STORYVILLE DETECTIVE
THE CASE OF THE GREEDY GRANNY
BY GEORGE McCLEMENTS

"Fractured fairy tale fans will love this. Adults will love the references to their favorite detective stories, and kids will enjoy figuring out the ending."

—Valerie Koehler, *Blue Willow Books*, Houston, TX

THE KING OF CAPRI
BY JEANETTE WINTERSON
ILLUSTRATED BY JANE RAY

"When the wind blows all of the rich and selfish King of Capri's possessions off his island and into poor Mrs. Jewel's yard, she becomes the Queen of Naples. Her generosity with this newfound wealth allows the king to see that there are things more precious than gold and silver."

—Beth Puffer, *Bank Street Bookstore*, New York, NY

KITTEN'S FIRST FULL MOON

BY KEVIN HENKES

"Oh, kitten! Henkes' black-and-white illustrations are delightful and tender. His writing, as always, is playful and endearing. Eager, courageous, and downright hungry, kitten learns she will always be provided for."
—Jessica Libero, *R. J. Julia Booksellers*, Madison, CT

KNUFFLE BUNNY
A CAUTIONARY TALE

BY MO WILLEMS

"Mo Willems—author of *Don't Let the Pigeon Drive the Bus*—has done it again! With terrific illustrations and an endearing story, this will be an absolute favorite. There is something about being able to relate to a character not yet capable of talking and the eventual triumph of speech."
—Mary Gleysteen, *Eagle Harbor Book Company*, Bainbridge Island, WA

MISTER SEAHORSE

BY ERIC CARLE

"Mister Seahorse discovers that he is only one of many
good fathers who care for their eggs and babies in a most
surprising way. As children are reassured of fatherly
devotion, they are learning little-known, fascinating facts
about nature. Carle's bold paper collage illustrations are
a wonderful treat."
—**Barbara Siepker**, *The Cottage Book Shop*, Glen Arbor, MI

OLIVIA...AND THE MISSING TOY

BY IAN FALCONER

"Olivia is back! This time, Ian Falconer has surpassed
himself with a great mystery and even more incredible
illustrations."
—**Dallas Holmes**, *Vroman's Bookstore*, Pasadena, CA

ALSO BY IAN FALCONER:
Olivia and *Olivia Saves the Circus*

ORVILLE
A Dog Story
BY HAVEN KIMMEL
ILLUSTRATED BY ROBERT ANDREW PARKER

"In *Orville*, two of my favorite things meet, at last,
in book form—Haven Kimmel's prose and a sweet,
wonderful dog. Parts of Orville's tale just break your heart.
But, here's a hint: It all turns out well in the end!"
 —Jen Reynolds, *Joseph-Beth Booksellers*, Cincinnati, OH

PETE SEEGER'S
ABIYOYO RETURNS
BY PETE SEEGER AND PAUL DUBOIS JACOBS
ILLUSTRATED BY MICHAEL HAYS

"The Abiyoyo is magically brought back to help the
community build a dam so there will be water in the
summer for irrigation. Pete's message is that communities
that share good food and song accept differences and make
everyone welcome. What a sweet tale."
 —Marian Fleischman, *Sedalia Book & Toy*, Sedalia, MO

THE PIGEON FINDS A HOT DOG!
BY MO WILLEMS

"I think this wonderful title just might be better than Willems' *Don't Let the Pigeon Drive the Bus*. This pigeon is stubborn, but cool, and I am a fan!"

—Branwen Robbins, *Apple Valley Books*, Winthrop, ME

PLANTZILLA
BY JERDINE NOLAN
ILLUSTRATED BY DAVID CATROW

"When Mortimer adopts the class plant for the summer, he gets a little more than he bargained for in this wacky tale. It quickly grows to *Little Shop of Horrors* proportions and begins to dominate the household. The story is told entirely through letters, an always delightful format, and the detailed illustrations are hilarious."

—Kate McNally, *Bookshop Benicia*, Benicia, CA

THE QUILTMAKER'S GIFT

BY JEFF BRUMBEAU
ILLUSTRATED BY GAIL DE MARCKEN

"This is the most beautiful children's book I've seen in
a long time. The story about a greedy king and the true
meaning of wealth is wonderful and the illustrations are
exquisite. It is incredible how many different things one
sees each time a page is turned."

—**Susan Wasson**, *Bookworks*, Albuquerque, NM

RIDE

BY STEPHEN GAMMELL

"This is a colorful splash of a book about an all-out
war for backseat space during a long car ride. The
conflict accelerates, fueled by the children's high-octane
imaginations, until Gammell's uproarious illustrations and
prose slip the confines of this exuberant picture book."

—**Erik Carmer Barnum**, *The Northshire Bookstore*,
Manchester Center, VT

ROBOTS SLITHER

BY RYAN ANN HUNTER
ILLUSTRATED BY JULIA GORTON

"Beginning readers will welcome the illustrations and
simple rhyme in this book. And they will also appreciate
the extra sound bites of information nicely placed within
the colorful artwork. It's great to find such an accessible
book on such a hot topic."

   —Jody Fickes Shapiro, *Adventures for Kids*, Ventura, CA

SEVEN SCARY MONSTERS

BY MARY BETH LUNDGREN
ILLUSTRATED BY HOWARD FINE

"Playful language and charming illustrations make this
story—about ridding a bedroom of monsters—a book
parents and grandparents can read to young children
again and again with enthusiasm."

   —Charlotte Deon, *Pine Island Books and More!*,
Matlacha, FL

THE SISSY DUCKLING

BY HARVEY FIERSTEIN

ILLUSTRATED BY HENRY COLE

"Elmer is a sissy duckling, and proud of it. He likes to paint and put on puppet shows. The boys in his flock make fun of him, and his own father is ashamed of him for not acting like a regular drake. But the day comes when Elmer, who always knows he has value, proves his worth to everyone. Power to the sissies!"

—**Carolyn Sweeney**, *Chesterfield Books*, Chesterfield, MI

SNOW MUSIC

BY LYNNE RAE PERKINS

"What does winter sound like? In this artful, deceptively simple picture book, Lynne Rae Perkins has captured the oft-missed harmonies of a season—from the rumbling chorus of a passing snowplow to the 'jingle, huff, jingle, huff' of a dog trotting through the snow."

—**Alison Morris**, *Wellesley Booksmith*, Wellesley, MA

SOMETIMES I'M BOMBALOO

BY RACHEL VAIL
ILLUSTRATED BY YUMI HEO

"Sometimes you just get so mad, you just can't stand it and you just have to let it out. But, then, you get into trouble and have to go to your room. As Katie learns in this wonderful book, there will always be someone who still loves us for what and who we are."

—**Kathy Taber**, *Kids Ink Children's Bookstore,*
Indianapolis, IN

STONE SOUP

BY JON J MUTH

"The creator of *The Three Questions* has taken the folktale of *Stone Soup*, given it an Asian twist, and illustrated it with breathtakingly beautiful art. This timeless story of cooperation and sharing is given a Zen perspective that will dazzle both children and adults."

—**Betty Bennett**, *Bennett Books*, Wyckoff, NJ

TAKE ME OUT OF THE BATHTUB
AND OTHER SILLY DILLY SONGS
BY ALAN KATZ
ILLUSTRATED BY DAVID CATROW

"My co-workers and I have hardly been able to conduct business lately. We have been lying on the floor convulsive while singing the songs in the book. The illustrations by Catrow are absolutely wonderful."

—**Alicia Greis**, *Colorado College Bookstore*, Colorado Springs, CO

THE THREE PIGS
BY DAVID WIESNER

"Wiesner can always be counted upon to create unusual books. This is the story of those same three pigs—except when they leave the story and go on a short, but very imaginative adventure into other books! A triumph, and great for adults, too."

—**Carol Stoltz**, *Concord Bookshop*, Concord, MA

TOOT & PUDDLE
TOP OF THE WORLD
BY HOLLY HOBBIE

"Toot's off again, so, knowing what his best friend loves to do, Puddle hops trains, planes and bicycles until he finds Toot in a French café. Then, off they go to Nepal for the biggest adventure of them all. Complete with beautiful watercolor illustrations, this one should get you hooked on these irresistible characters!"
—Mary Fellow, *Annie Bloom's Bookstore*, Portland, OR

ALSO IN THE TOOT & PUDDLE SERIES:
Toot & Puddle, Toot & Puddle: You Are My Sunshine, Toot & Puddle: The New Friend, and more

THE TREE
BY DANA LYONS
ILLUSTRATED BY DAVID DANIOTH

"The illustrations are beautiful, the text is simple, and the message clear: It is our place to protect our natural resources. This book is very beautiful and moving."
—Julie Heidtman, *Page One*, Albuquerque, NM

WHEN LIGHTNING COMES IN A JAR
BY PATRICIA POLACCO

"If you have ever read any of Polacco's work, you
know that she always weaves a great tale involving
childhood stories full of love and warmth and lots of
relatives. This is no exception! A young girl learns from
her Gramma how to catch lightning in a jar at their
family reunion. What a wonderful family!"
    —**Monica Capra**, *Scott's Bookstore*, Mt. Vernon, WA

WHO NEEDS DONUTS?
BY MARK ALAN STAMATY

"I hardly know where to start praising this fun read.
Stamaty is a brilliant illustrator, and this book is stuffed
with visual jokes, puns, and bizarre hidden messages. He's
also an extraordinarily whimsical, wild, and entertaining
storyteller, who combines an outrageously original sense
of the ridiculous with a basic and sublime understanding
of what kids and grown-ups all 'need.' Now republished,
another generation of kids (and adults) can have all the
fun, too."
    —**Susan Avery**, *Ariel Booksellers*, New Paltz, NY

WILD ABOUT BOOKS

BY JUDY SIERRA
ILLUSTRATED BY MARC BROWN

"Ever wonder what would happen if a bookmobile mistakenly showed up at the town zoo? This is the premise of *Wild About Books*, where all the animals discover the joy of books and, in their own unique ways, become avid readers. The fanciful illustrations and clever wording make this a book you will want to read again and again."

—Betty Bennett, *Bennett Books*, Wyckoff, NJ

WISH, CHANGE, FRIEND

BY IAN WHYBROW
ILLUSTRATED BY TIPHANIE BEEKE

"I adore this book and think it's a gem. Little Pig is an endearing character, and his discovery of the power of words and the joys of friendship are charmingly presented. The book is a natural for wonderful discussions with youngsters."

—Betsey Detwiler, *Buttonwood Books & Toys*, Cohasset, MA

YOU'RE ALL MY FAVORITES

BY SAM MCBRATNEY
ILLUSTRATED BY ANITA JERAM

"This great children's book about Mommy and Daddy
Bear and their three cubs will reassure all children in a
family that they are loved."

—Cissie Roth, *Diana's Bookstore*, Elkin, NC

The Three Questions cover illustration, copyright © 2002 by Jon J Muth

PICTURE BOOKS FOR OLDER CHILDREN

Beth Puffer, *Bank Street Bookstore*, New York, NY

JUST BECAUSE A CHILD HAS LEARNED TO READ DOESN'T mean he or she has outgrown picture books. Though one usually thinks of reading picture books to a child snuggled on your lap, they can also be striking and accessible sources of information for both children and adults. Whether a child is interested in history, sports, science, or the world around them, a picture book can start them on a journey of discovery.

The combination of words and illustrations in a book like *When Marian Sang*, by Pam Muñoz Ryan, makes the reader feel Marian Anderson's determination and the power of her story. Text alone would not allow the child to be a part of this moment in history. Similarly, in *How the Amazon Queen Fought the Prince of Egypt*, by Tamara Bower, the story of Queen Serpot is enhanced by the hieroglyphic translations on each page. The notes and glossaries in such books add yet another level of information.

A picture book told through the eyes of a child can make the story more meaningful to the young reader. In *Freedom on the Menu*, by Carol Boston Weatherford, a young girl watches her older brother and sister get involved in the civil rights movement. Though she may not understand all that is happening, she knows that it will change their lives.

Chico, the son of migrant workers in *First Day in Grapes*, by L. King Perez, tells of his unique experience as his family constantly moves with the crops while exploring the universal experience of standing up to a bully.

One doesn't normally think of math when speaking of picture books and yet a book like *Sir Cumference and the First Round Table*, by Cindy Neuschwander, can introduce geometry while telling of King Arthur and his knights. In *You Can't Buy a Dinosaur with a Dime*, author Harriet Ziefert uses Pete and his money jar to address the issue of spending and saving.

While a picture book may make only passing references to a difficult subject it can open the way to deeper discussion. In *The Lily Cupboard*, by Shulamith Levey Oppenheim, a young girl tells of being hidden during the Holocaust, though the reason she must not be found is only touched upon. Books like this provide a perfect discussion starter for all manner of tough topics.

As the selection of picture books for older readers increases, parents, teachers, and librarians are provided with an excellent way to help children understand the world as it was, as it is, and as it can be.

ADVENTURES OF RILEY
AMAZON RIVER RESCUE
BY AMANDA LUMRY & LAURA HURWITZ
ILLUSTRATED BY SARAH McINTYRE

"Riley visits different regions of the world to explore the area wildlife and to learn about the culture and environmental aspects of that particular region. Colorfully presented, combining illustrations with photography, this is great for the classroom, and great for the future of world conservation."

—**David Henkes**, *University Book Store*, Bellevue, WA

ALSO IN THE ADVENTURES OF RILEY SERIES:
Dolphins in Danger, Tigers in Terai, Mission to Madagascar, and *Safari in South Africa*

AMERICA'S CHAMPION SWIMMER: GERTRUDE EDERLE
BY DAVID A. ADLER
ILLUSTRATED BY TERRY WIDENER

"This one passed the goose bumps test! Children will cheer, and girls will feel especially proud of this athlete who won three medals at the 1924 Paris Olympics and went on to do what no woman had ever done—swim the English Channel. That she did it in two hours less than any man made reporters declare that the myth of the weaker sex was 'shattered and shattered forever.' Widener's colorful paintings capture the spirit of the stirring text. Bravo!"

—**Linda Bubon**, *Women & Children First,* Chicago, IL

THE BEE-MAN OF ORN

BY FRANK R. STOCKTON
ILLUSTRATED BY P. J. LYNCH

"Written at the turn of the century, and then illustrated by Sendak in 1964, one of my very favorite books has been reissued again! It's about the classic argument of nature vs. nurture, and nature wins."

—**Judy Hamel**, *The Children's Corner Bookshop*,
Spokane, WA

BRUNDIBAR

RETOLD BY TONY KUSHNER
ILLUSTRATED BY MAURICE SENDAK

"*Brundibar* is based on a Czech opera for children that was performed fifty-five times by the children of Terezin, the Nazi concentration camp. This lyrical, Old World story—like *Stone Soup*—is fun to read aloud and beautifully illustrated, too. It's sure to earn a place among your favorite classics."

—**Katie Snodgrass**, *Square Books*, Oxford, MS

D IS FOR DEMOCRACY
A Citizen's Alphabet
⁂ BY ELISSA GRODIN
ILLUSTRATED BY VICTOR JUHASZ

"*D Is for Democracy* reminds children (and adults) of the principles our country was built upon. It is a nonpartisan reminder of the importance of participation in our government. A treat for election—or any other—year!"
—Kay Vincent, *Bohannons' Books With a Past,*
Georgetown, KY

THE DINOSAURS OF WATERHOUSE HAWKINS
⁂ BY BARBARA KERLEY
ILLUSTRATED BY BRIAN SELZNICK

"This stunning picture book reveals the amazing true story of an unknown figure in the history of dinosaur research. A brilliant, fascinating book!"
—Marianne Harper, *Brystone Children's Books,*
Fort Worth, TX

ELLINGTON WAS NOT A STREET

BY NTOZAKE SHANGE
ILLUSTRATED BY KADIR NELSON

"The lines of text set on the pages of this book are a subtle drumbeat to the music of the book's illustrations, and the author's poem is a testament to some of the pillars of the African-American community. It recalls a time when streets were not named for black people, and the individuals who changed that world."

—**Melissa Manlove**, *The Storyteller*, Lafayette, CA

THE FIRST FEUD BETWEEN THE MOUNTAIN AND THE SEA

BY LYNN PLOURDE
ILLUSTRATED BY JIM SOLLERS

"A great story with an even greater lesson—that beauty is not a treasure to be hoarded, but a blessing to be shared."

—**Rita Moran**, *Apple Valley Books*, Winthrop, ME

FREEDOM ON THE MENU
THE GREENSBORO SIT-INS
BY CAROLE BOSTON WEATHERFORD
ILLUSTRATED BY JEROME LAGARRIGUE

"*Freedom on the Menu* fills that hard-to-fit niche: books that make historical events understandable for young readers. By portraying the world and its changing events through the eyes of eight-year-old Connie, Weatherford makes the Civil Rights movement approachable. Lagarrigue's softly etched paintings bring feeling to a harsh but inspiring subject."
 —Rosemary Pugliese, *Quail Ridge Books*, Raleigh, NC

HARVESTING HOPE
THE STORY OF CESAR CHAVEZ
BY KATHLEEN KRULL
ILLUSTRATED BY YUYI MORALES

"Cesar Chavez organized migrant farm workers in California and fought for human rights and better lives for migrant farm workers. His legacy extends well beyond his state's borders. A beautiful book."
 —Jenifer Ross, *City Lights Books*, San Francisco, CA

IF THE WORLD WERE A VILLAGE
A Book About the World's People
BY DAVID J. SMITH
ILLUSTRATED BY SHELAGH ARMSTRONG

"This book is so cool! If the world consisted of 100 people in one small village, how many of those people would have computers? Have enough to eat? Be able to read? Smith makes global issues accessible to all. Perfect to introduce children to the world around them, especially at this time."

—**Nikki Mutch**, *UConn Co-op*, Storrs, CT

LITTLE LIT
Strange Stories for Strange Kids
EDITED BY ART SPIEGELMAN & FRANÇOISE MOULY

"Maurice Sendak, Jules Feiffer, and a story by David Sedaris illustrated by Ian Falconer— do I really need to say any more? This book is so much fun. A giant picture book for the comic book lover and for the all the strange little kiddies out there who love it when the ordinary gets turned inside out and becomes extraordinary!"

—**Jill Bailey**, *Book People*, Austin, TX

MICHAEL ROSEN'S SAD BOOK

BY MICHAEL ROSEN
ILLUSTRATED BY QUENTIN BLAKE

"Rosen writes with moving honesty about the death of his son, but Blake's quirky illustrations are what save this story from being too dire and bleak. Art and text work together to weave a truly remarkable book that is the perfect starting point for a discussion about what troubles a child."
      —Elizabeth Reynolds, *Norwich Bookstore*, Norwich, VT

MY BROTHER MARTIN
A SISTER REMEMBERS GROWING UP WITH THE REV. DR. MARTIN LUTHER KING JR.

BY CHRISTINE KING FARRIS
ILLUSTRATED BY CHRIS SOENTPIET

"Dr. King's older sister, Christine, relates how the sometimes painful experience of growing up in the segregated South of the 1920s set her family, and her brother, Martin, in particular, on the path to leadership in the Civil Rights Movement."
      —Robin Green-Cary, *Sibanye Inc.*, Baltimore, MD

PATROL
AN AMERICAN SOLDIER IN VIETNAM
BY WALTER DEAN MYERS
COLLAGES BY ANN GRIFALCONI

"This book is stunning, powerful, and (unfortunately) will always be timely. Myers describes the reality of being a soldier: the fear, the ambiguity, and the sadness. The collage art of Vietnamese jungles and villages is hauntingly beautiful."

—**Will Peters**, *Annie Bloom's Books,* Portland, OR

UNWITTING WISDOM
AN ANTHOLOGY OF AESOP'S FABLES
RETOLD AND ILLUSTRATED BY HELEN WARD

"Elegant and sophisticated illustrations accompany a dozen of Aesop's most familiar fables. The oversize format makes it great for sharing with a large group. Just gorgeous."

—**Carol Moyer**, *Quail Ridge Books*, Raleigh, NC

WESLANDIA

BY PAUL FLEISCHMAN
ILLUSTRATED BY KEVIN HAWKES

"An innovative story about a young boy who, shunned
by his peers, taps into his own creativity. He establishes a
new food crop, a new language, and, in the end, a new
civilization. Very highly recommended."

—Joseph Lappie, *Danner's Books*, Muncie, IN

WHEN MARIAN SANG

BY PAM MUÑOZ RYAN
ILLUSTRATED BY BRIAN SELZNICK

"Ryan's words and Selznick's art powerfully combine
to bring to life the story of Marian Anderson's incredible
triumph in the late 1930s: finally being allowed to
sing before an integrated audience on the Lincoln
Memorial steps."

—Candace Moreno, *San Marino Toy and Book Shoppe*,
San Marino, CA

THE WOLVES IN THE WALLS

BY NEIL GAIMAN

ILLUSTRATED BY DAVE McKEAN

"Before Neil Gaiman became well-known and widely appreciated as a novelist, he and illustrator Dave McKean worked some real magic in the graphic novel/comics field. McKean combines scratchy, primitive lines with photographs and computer-treated images to create a stirring visual narrative that accompanies and complements Gaiman's subtly layered story. Now that's a kids' book for adults."

—**Michael F. Russo**, *St. Mark's Bookshop*, New York, NY

CHAPTER BOOKS

Josie Leavitt and Elizabeth Bluemle,
Flying Pig Children's Books, Charlotte, VT

CHAPTER BOOKS HAVE ALWAYS BEEN SPECIAL TO CHILDREN. As the early struggles of reading turn to fluency, young readers are excited to "graduate" from easy readers to longer books with chapters. More confident in their newly learned skills, children are eager and able to dive into stories for longer periods of time.

The term "chapter book" has a specialized meaning in the world of children's literature. Any book with chapters is, of course, by definition a chapter book, but publishers designate as chapter books those transitional books that lie—in length and difficulty—between easy readers and novels. So popular are these books that a whole cottage industry has sprung up as a subset of children's publishing.

A good chapter book engages children on their level, challenges them as readers, and promises success because it's just the right length. Some recent customer favorites are the *Magic Tree House* series by Mary Pope Osborne, *The Secrets of Droon* series by Tony Abbott, the *A to Z Mysteries* series by Ron Roy, *The Time Warp Trio* series by Jon Scieszka, *The Cobble Street Cousins* series by Cynthia

Rylant, *The Zack Files* by Dan Greenburg, and the *Dragon Slayers' Academy* series by Kate McMullan.

In addition to books and series published especially for the transitional reading market, there are wonderful books, both classic and new, that also enchant emerging readers. Books like Richard and Florence Atwater's *Mr. Popper's Penguins*, Ruth Stiles Gannett's *My Father's Dragon*, Scott Corbett's *The Lemonade Trick*, Oliver Butterworth's *The Enormous Egg*, Johanna Hurwitz's *Pee-Wee's Tale*, and a myriad of books by Dick King-Smith regularly fly off the shelves.

Slightly longer, more challenging chapter books make wonderful read-alouds for families with chapter-book–aged children. Often, children return to these books on their own a little down the road; having heard them aloud helps anchor the stories and characters in their minds. Some of our childhood favorites that keep going strong are *The Cricket in Times Square* by George Selden, *Ramona the Pest* (and anything else) by Beverly Cleary, *Ronia, the Robber's Daughter* by Astrid Lindgren, and *Homer Price* by Robert McCloskey. The beauty of good chapter books is that they last—not only through time, but in the minds of children who discover them for the first time.

BETSY-TACY

BY MAUD HART LOVELACE
ILLUSTRATED BY LOIS LENSKI

"The *Betsy-Tacy* series remains one of my best childhood memories. My mom got me hooked on them and I devoured each one from Betsy at age five through her wedding. Timeless in their tales about friendship, it is a joy to see this series back in print for more kids to inhale."
                    —**Sheri Kraft**, *Alibi Books*, Glenview, IL

ALSO IN THE BETSY-TACY SERIES:
Betsy-Tacy and Tib, Betsy and Tacy Go Over the Big Hill, Betsy and Tacy Go Downtown, Heaven to Betsy, Betsy in Spite of Herself, and more

THE BOOKSTORE MOUSE

BY PEGGY CHRISTIAN
ILLUSTRATED BY GARY LIPPINCOTT

"Perhaps one of my family's favorite books of all time, it's the story of a bookstore mouse, an illiterate cat, and an adventure in words. There's a giant named Jargon, a dragon named Censor, and a scribe named Cervantes. A great read-aloud for all ages."
                    —**Nancy Tebeau**, *Not Just for Kids Bookstore*,
                    Wake Forest, NC

THE CHAMELEON WORE CHARTREUSE
A CHET GECKO MYSTERY
BY BRUCE HALE

"Meet Chet Gecko, fourth-grader at Emerson Hicky Elementary. When Billy Chameleon disappears from school one day, Chet must battle a Gila monster and escape certain death by chlorination before he uncovers Billy's trail!"
—**Libby Alison Richmond**, *Inklings Bookshop*, Yakima, WA

ALSO IN THE CHET GECKO SERIES:
The Malted Falcon; This Gum for Hire; The Mystery of Mr. Nice; Farewell, My Lunchbag; and more

FREDDY THE DETECTIVE
BY WALTER R. BROOKS
ILLUSTRATED BY KURT WIESE

"*Library Journal* says: 'Freddy is simply one of the greatest characters in children's literature!' And I agree. Freddy is a multi-talented pig: detective, editor, magician, and more. He is sassy and sagacious, a lover of language and a true wit, like his creator Walter Brooks, who served on the editorial board of *The New Yorker* in the 1930s."
—**Bobby Tichenor**, *Annie Bloom's*, Portland, OR

OTHER FREDDY ADVENTURES INCLUDE:
Freddy the Magician, Freddy and the Ignormus, Freddy Goes Camping, Freddy and the Men from Mars, and more

GOONEY BIRD AND THE ROOM MOTHER
BY LOIS LOWRY
ILLUSTRATED BY MIDDY THOMAS

"Like Mrs. Pidgeon's second grade class, 'Suddenly...' is all we need to hear to sit up straight, pay attention, and prepare for the full, delighted laugh Gooney Bird brings us in every chapter. In this case the story turns on the shortage of room mothers and Gooney Bird's ingenious solution, kept just out of view until the final pages. The subtext is children seeing ways to lead, and taking the responsibility to do so."
   —**Carol B. Chittenden**, *Eight Cousins*, Falmouth, MA

THE SEQUEL TO THIS BOOK: *Gooney Bird Greene*

THE IRON GIANT
A STORY IN FIVE NIGHTS
BY TED HUGHES

"Reissued in a 30th anniversary edition, this story brings together humor, adventure and drama in a timely message of peace that is accessible to children."
   —**Jeanie Stoddard**, *Politics and Prose*, Washington DC

JENNY AND THE CAT CLUB
BY ESTHER AVERILL

"I was so, so excited to see this title reissued! I grew up with Jenny (a small black cat with a red scarf) and her friends and all their adventures. This is a great story collection, with some illustrations—perfect for kids who are trying to read on their own, and great for bedtime stories."
—**Nicki Leone**, *Bristol Books*, Wilmington, NC

ALSO IN THE JENNY'S CAT CLUB SERIES:
The School for Cats, The Hotel Cat, Captains of the City Streets, Jenny Goes to Sea, Jenny's Birthday Book, and *Jenny's Moonlight Adventure*

JUDY MOODY SAVES THE WORLD!
BY MEGAN MCDONALD
ILLUSTRATED BY PETER REYNOLDS

"The third installment in the Judy Moody series is perfect for second and third graders. Judy is on a tear about recycling and the environment! A fun read and a spunky little heroine."
—**Diane Smith-Hill**, *A Children's Place*, Portland, OR

ALSO IN THE JUDY MOODY SERIES:
Judy Moody Declares Independence, Judy Moody Gets Famous, Judy Moody Predicts The Future, and *Judy Moody, M.D.: The Doctor Is In!*

THE MOUSE OF AMHERST

BY ELIZABETH SPIRES
ILLUSTRATED BY CLAIRE A. NIVOLA

"A charming tale for ages eight to eighty! Emily Dickinson leaves bits of poetry around the house, and a mouse living in the wainscoting writes poetry back!"

—Wyatt and Nancy Young, *Drummer Boy Books*, Ligonier, PA

RED RIDIN'
IN THE HOOD
And Other Cuentos

BY PATRICIA SANTOS MARCANTONIO
ILLUSTRATED BY RENATO ALARCAO

"Fairy tales with the flavor of Mexico! My favorite was 'The Three Chicharrones,' but then I laughed through 'The Sleeping Beauty.' Much more realistic than the originals, with a great twist."

—Ellen Perry, *Browsing Bison Books*, Deer Lodge, MT

SPECIAL GIFTS
THE COBBLE STREET COUSINS
BY CYNTHIA RYLANT

ILLUSTRATED BY WENDY ANDERSON HALPERIN

"Good, wholesome stories of the plans and adventures of three girl cousins."

—**Sandra Soss & Colby Beutel**, *Sweet Pea Books*, Chicago, IL

ALSO IN THE COBBLE STREET COUSINS SERIES:
In Aunt Lucy's Kitchen, A Little Shopping, Some Good News, Summer Party, and *Wedding of Flowers*

STANLEY, FLAT AGAIN!
BY JEFF BROWN

ILLUSTRATED BY SCOTT NASH

"This silly series about a boy who's only a half-inch thick after a mishap with a bulletin board will appeal to the whimsical imagination of kids and adults alike!"

—**Jill Ogata**, *Bookworks*, Albuquerque, NM

ALSO IN THE FLAT STANLEY SERIES:
Flat Stanley, Stanley and the Magic Lamp, Invisible Stanley, Stanley in Space, and *Stanley's Christmas Adventure*

TIM IN DANGER

 BY EDWARD ARDIZZONE

"A grand adventure series written by Edward Ardizzone between 1936 and 1977. Brave little Tim sets out to sea, having one triumphant adventure after another. The illustrations are fresh and fine, and the writing is simple and fun."

—**Elizabeth Bluemle**, *Flying Pig Children's Books,*
Charlotte, VT

ALSO IN THE TIM BOOK SERIES:
Tim and Ginger, Tim's Friend Towser, Tim to the Rescue, Little Tim and the Brave Sea Captain, and more

"Petra took off on her own. She passed the Degas dancers, the big painting made completely of dots, the Monet haystacks and bridges, and headed into the older works."

Illustration copyright © 2004 by Brett Helquist from *Chasing Vermeer*, by Blue Balliett

MIDDLE GRADE

Judy Nelson, *Mrs. Nelson's Toy & Book Shop*, LaVerne, CA

MIDDLE-GRADE CHILDREN, AGES EIGHT TO TWELVE, HAVE A voracious appetite for reading. In part, their hunger for books is fueled by newfound independence. They are, often for the first time, selecting their own reading material, and unlike teen readers, aren't bogged down with assigned reading for school. Middle-grade readers may have suggested reading lists, but are given a lot more latitude. As a result, they enjoy the responsibility of choosing titles themselves and being able to discuss them with their peers. Perhaps it's that peer input that causes certain titles to be deemed "girl books" or "boy books." Though girls tend to read both, most boys won't even touch the so-called girl titles like *The Meanest Doll in the World* and *Olivia Kidney*.

The interests of middle-grade children range from adventure and fantasy (especially in a series format) to history, mystery, and sheer silliness. Classics such as *James and the Giant Peach* (and other books by Roald Dahl), *Charlotte's Web*, by E. B. White, the *Fudge* series by Judy Blume, and the *Ramona Quimby* series by Beverly Cleary are still selling well to a new generation of readers. Books that contain what I call gross-out humor such as *The Day*

My Butt Went Psycho! and scary books such as the classic *Scary Stories to Tell in the Dark* series are among the most popular with boys in this age group.

Fortunately, fantasy books, which make up a large portion of middle-grade titles, appeal to both sexes. I give credit to J. K. Rowling for revitalizing the genre. In the wake of her Harry Potter success, a slew of new fantasies, including *Eragon, Molly Moon's Incredible Book of Hypnotism, Dragon Rider, The City of Ember,* and Lemony Snicket's *A Series of Unfortunate Events* have emerged. These are all wonderful reads. However, it's important to remember that although middle-grade readers are empowered by the ability to choose their reading material, they are still young and can definitely benefit from adult guidance.

BECAUSE OF WINN-DIXIE

BY KATE DiCAMILLO

"India Opal is one of the strongest, most sensitive and sensible heroines since Scout in *To Kill a Mockingbird*. Kate DiCamillo's first novel is a marvel. Not to be missed!"

—**Collette Morgan**, *Wild Rumpus*, Minneapolis, MN

BECOMING NAOMI LEÓN

BY PAM MUÑOZ RYAN

"Naomi León Outlaw is an immediately likable character, and you will be rooting for her to find herself, her voice, and her father. The author has written a beautiful, intense book full of family and friends and imbued with the rich culture of Mexico. This book and Naomi will touch your heart."

—**Jill Bailey**, *BookPeople*, Austin, TX

BUNNICULA
A RABBIT-TALE OF MYSTERY
BY DEBORAH AND JAMES HOWE
ILLUSTRATED BY ALAN DANIEL

"For child as well as parent appeal, it doesn't get any better (or scarier!) than *Bunnicula*. Kids will know it couldn't really happen—a Vampire rabbit?—but the possibility appeals to their lust for creepiness. The wordplay and family dynamics ring true with grownups, and as a read-aloud, the opportunities for voices brings out the thespian in any parent."

—**Cheryl McKeon**, *Third Place Books*,
Lake Forest Park, WA

CHARLIE BONE AND THE TIME TWISTER
BY JENNY NIMMO

"All your favorite (and most unfavorite) characters are here in this wonderful sequel to *Midnight for Charlie Bone*, as well as some new ones you'll enjoy. I love this series."

—**Julie Heidtman**, *Page One Bookstore*,
Albuquerque, NM

ALSO IN THE CHARLIE BONE SERIES:
Charlie Bone and the Invisible Boy, Charlie Bone and the Castle of Mirrors, and *Midnight for Charlie Bone*

CHASING VERMEER

﹏ BY BLUE BALLIETT
ILLUSTRATED BY BRETT HELQUIST

"What a fun book this was to read. Two sixth-graders,
a creative teacher, stolen art, letters written in secret code,
and a lot of seemingly unrelated clues had me guessing all
along the way."

—**Kimberly A. Hughes**, *Village Bookstore*,
Menomonee Falls, WI

CHILDREN OF THE LAMP
THE AKHENATEN ADVENTURE

﹏ BY P.B. KERR

"This book has great promise! This story of twelve-year-
old twins who discover they are djinn takes you beyond
just the realm of magic and into the ideas of good versus
evil throughout the world."

—**Cris Walrath**, *Browsing Bison Books*, Deer Lodge, MT

THE CITY OF EMBER
BY JEANNE DuPRAU

"A cautionary tale (wrapped up in a mystery-adventure) of what could happen to our world if we squander our resources. Read it with your children, and it will spur discussions about responsibility, citizenship, death, and selfishness. Wonderful!"
—**Sarah Carr**, *McIntyre's Fine Books*, Pittsboro, NC

CRISPIN
THE CROSS OF LEAD
BY AVI

"Avi has done it again! He has created a story of interest to a wide range of ages. We are taken to Medieval England, and through the eyes of a serf, we see the effects of the plague, the social order of the day, and a political change for equality. Not to worry; the story is full of intrigue and excitement!"
—**Jen Butler-Brown**, *Grass Roots Books & Music*, Corvallis, OR

DOUBLE FUDGE

BY JUDY BLUME

"Hurrah! Fudge is back! And he is better and funnier
than ever! But be warned: It might be that Fudge has
met his match in a newly discovered cousin who 'stole' his
name. Double the Fudge means double the laughs, and
you'll be laughing out loud!"

—**Deborah Woolsey**, *Dragonwings Bookstore,*
Waupaca, WI

ALSO IN THE FUDGE SERIES:
*Tales of a Fourth Grade Nothing, Otherwise Known as Sheila the
Great, Superfudge,* and *Fudge-a-Mania.*

DRAGON RIDER

BY CORNELIA FUNKE

"This is a wonderful adventure story about dragons
trying to find a safe place to live away from humans. It's
a story—filled with mythical animals and a human boy—
that tells how they bond and help each other out. Children
will love this tale."

—**Lee Musgjerd**, *Lee's Book Emporium*, Glasgow, MT

THE END OF THE BEGINNING
BEING THE ADVENTURES OF A SMALL SNAIL (AND AN EVEN SMALLER ANT)
BY AVI
ILLUSTRATED BY TRICIA TUSA

"Avi's story is a charming tale, featuring an ant and a snail on an adventure. The format of this book, as well as the illustrations by beloved artist Tricia Tusa, make this a timeless classic, perfect for all ages."

—**Elizabeth Reynolds**, *Norwich Bookstore*, Norwich, VT

GRANNY TORRELLI MAKES SOUP
BY SHARON CREECH

"This may be master storyteller and Newbery Medal-winner Sharon Creech's finest offering to young readers yet. Over zesty Italian cooking, Granny Torrelli offers insight to Rosie by telling tales of her own childhood friend Pedro. It is simple wisdom told with brilliant charm."

—**Mary Brice**, *Tattered Cover Bookstore*, Denver, CO

THE GREAT GOOD THING
BY RODERICK TOWNLEY
ILLUSTRATED BY STEPHANIE ANDERSON

"The plot is absolutely unique, and I love the way the author plays with the fairy tale genre: Princess Sylvie and her friends know they're characters in a book and that their job is to entertain The Reader. This is the best book I've read in a very long time."

—Katherine Bryk, *The Learned Owl Book Shop*, Hudson, OH

THE GREEN KNOWE CHRONICLES
BY L. M. BOSTON
ILLUSTRATED BY PETER BOSTON

"A series of five reissued classics from the early fifties, great for fans of Lemony Snicket, Eva Ibbotson, and J. K. Rowling. These are great fantasies featuring a cavernous old mansion, some magic, and great characters to get to know."

—Jennifer Brenninger, *Doylestown Bookshop*, Doylestown, PA

IN THE GREEN KNOWE CHRONICLES:
The Children of Green Knowe, Treasure of Green Knowe, The River at Green Knowe, A Stranger at Green Knowe, An Enemy at Green Knowe, and *The Stones of Green Knowe*

GREGOR AND THE PROPHECY OF BANE

BY SUZANNE COLLINS

"Gregor the Overlander is back and, once again, he follows his baby sister, Boots, this time through a doorway in Central Park to the Underland. There, he's destined to confront a mysterious white Rat King. This exciting sequel is even better than the first book. I couldn't put it down."

—**Joanne R. Fritz**, *Chester County Book & Music Company*, West Chester, PA

ALSO IN THE UNDERLAND CHRONICLES:
Gregor the Overlander and *Gregor and the Curse of the Warmbloods*

THE HAUNTING OF GRANITE FALLS

BY EVA IBBOTSON
ILLUSTRATED BY KEVIN HAWKES

"This is a gentle story about friendly ghosts who are very disconcerted to have their castle moved from Ireland to Texas! What a delightful storyteller Ibbotson is. Great fun for seven- to ten-year-olds."

—**Jane Stroh**, *The Bookstore*, Glen Ellyn, IL

HOLES

BY LOUIS SACHAR

"I love to recommend this because it really makes
kids think. They learn about crime, punishment, and
redemption, and just how long it takes to dig a hole and
how to get out of any hole they have dug for themselves."
— **Margaret Petteruto**, *San Marino Toy and Book Shoppe,*
San Marino, CA

HOOT

BY CARL HIAASEN

"Hiaasen hasn't written down to his youthful audience;
he's just written, and it works beautifully. He deftly juggles
the 'work-within-the-system/subvert-the-system' points of
view, and has done a great job with the kids, including the
bully. What a great book."
— **Susan Scott**, *The Secret Garden Bookshop*, Seattle, WA

A HOUSE CALLED AWFUL END
BOOK ONE OF THE EDDIE DICKINS TRILOGY
BY PHILIP ARDAGH
ILLUSTRATED BY DAVID ROBERTS

"All you fans of Mr. Snicket and Mr. Dahl, here you go! Mr. Ardagh is here with a new series about kids persevering despite some dire straits. Here's the first ridiculous, witty, and fun installment. Enjoy!"

—**Carol Schweppe**, *Hicklebee's*, San Jose, CA

ALSO IN THE EDDIE DICKINS TRILOGY:
Dreadful Acts and *Terrible Times*

IDA B...AND HER PLANS TO MAXIMIZE FUN, AVOID DISASTER, AND (POSSIBLY) SAVE THE WORLD
BY KATHERINE HANNIGAN

"A fearless and joyful homeschooled ten-year-old, Ida B becomes a surly, withdrawn student when she is forced to attend school after her mother is diagnosed with cancer. Still, with the steadfast love of her family, the quiet support of her remarkable teacher, and her own inner fortitude and considerable insight, Ida B remains wonder-filled and triumphant."

—**Coral Jordan**, *Harry W. Schwartz Bookshop*, Mequon, WI

INKHEART
BY CORNELIA FUNKE

"If you thought *The Thief Lord* was great—try out Funke's latest. Mo is a bookbinder who loves books and his only family, a young daughter. They are uprooted from a somewhat eccentric life and dragged on an unprecedented adventure of books, thugs, Italy, magic, mystery and intrigue. For any true book lover, this book is it. I dare you to read it aloud."

—**Jennifer Lawton,** *Just Books,* Greenwich, CT

THE SEQUEL TO INKHEART: *Inkspell*

JUST ELLA
BY MARGARET PETERSON HADDIX

"Beginning where 'happily ever after' left off, this is the 'true' story of Cinderella. Ella quickly discovers that life with Prince Charming isn't what she'd expected and that being treated like royalty isn't what she wants after all. This book is very smart and very funny—including a scene where Ella explains what really happened the night of the ball in a vain attempt to dispel fairy tale superstitions. A must read!"

—**Gina Guilinger,** *Bailey/Coy Books,* Seattle, WA

LEAPING BEAUTY
AND OTHER ANIMAL FAIRY TALES
BY GREGORY MAGUIRE
ILLUSTRATED BY CHRIS L. DEMAREST

"In Maguire's style of retelling age-old stories, this collection is full of laughs and meant for all ages. Each tale is fun to read and to compare with your memory of the original."

—**Carl Wichman**, *Varsity Mart*, Fargo, ND

LIONBOY
BY ZIZOU CORDER

"Charlie's quest to rescue his kidnapped, famous scientist parents leads to a meeting with a fabulous circus. This is a kid's dream book…a boy on his own on a hero's quest joins with perhaps the most exciting circus in children's literature. And, oh yeah, he can talk to lions!"

—**Dana Harper**, *Brystone Children's Books*,
Fort Worth, TX

ALSO IN THE LIONBOY TRILOGY:
Lionboy: The Chase and *Lionboy: The Truth*

LOSER
BY JERRY SPINELLI

"This was riveting from the very first page. I *highly* recommend this to any parent, and especially one who has a son. It had me laughing and crying. This book cuts to the core of what it is like to be a thoughtful and sensitive young man in our sometimes cruel and confusing world. This is one of the best books I have read in years."
—**Tom Montan**, *Copperfield's Books*, Sebastopol, CA

LOVE THAT DOG
BY SHARON CREECH

"'I don't want to because boys don't write poetry. Girls do.' So begins the saga between young writer, Jack, and his encouraging teacher, Miss Stretchbery. This short novel, written in poetry form, allows us to follow along as Jack finds pride in writing. What a gift this book is to aspiring authors and their teachers."
—**Marilyn Smith**, *Hawley-Cooke Booksellers*, Louisville, KY

MAGYK
SEPTIMUS HEAP, BOOK ONE
BY ANGIE SAGE
ILLUSTRATED BY MARK ZUG

"This is one that is sure to please *Harry Potter* and *Edge Chronicle* fans! Telling the story of an anonymous, hidden princess who is pursued by an evil wizard, this book is filled with adventure, fantasy, and fun."

—**Kathleen Raymond**, *Davis-Kidd Booksellers*, Memphis, TN

THE MEANEST DOLL
IN THE WORLD
BY ANN M. MARTIN AND LAURA GODWIN
ILLUSTRATED BY BRIAN SELZNICK

"In the sequel to the charming *The Doll People*, dolls Annabelle and Tiffany Funcraft return for the romp, but, this time, they travel to the exciting world of school, where they encounter Mean Mimi, who is determined to rule all of Dollkind. Will the world ever be safe for dolls again? This nonstop adventure from a doll's-eye view comes alive with Selznick's rich black-and-white illustrations."

—**Morgan McMillian**, *Politics and Prose Bookstore and Coffeehouse*, Washington, DC

MOLLY MOON'S INCREDIBLE BOOK OF HYPNOTISM

BY GEORGIA BYNG

"Not much is going Molly Moon's way until the day she finds a book on hypnotism stuck on the wrong shelf at the library. Suddenly, her true talents become apparent, and she finds herself on the path to fame and fortune—and quite a bit of misfortune as well. Funny and touching."

—**Kristine Kaufman**, *The Snow Goose Bookstore*,
Stanwood, WA

ALSO IN THE MOLLY MOON SERIES:
Molly Moon Stops the World and *Molly Moon's Hypnotic Time Travel Adventure*

THE MONSTERS OF MORLEY MANOR
A Madcap Adventure

BY BRUCE COVILLE

"How can anyone put down a book when the first sentence is 'If Sarah hadn't put the monkey in the bathtub, we might never have had to help the monsters get big.' A wonderful adventure with determined, clever aliens and a spunky brother-and-sister team who possess great courage, loyalty, and humor."

—**Janis Irvine**, *The Book Bin*, Northbrook, IL

THE MOUSE AND HIS CHILD

BY RUSSELL HOBAN
ILLUSTRATED BY DAVID SMALL

"Originally published in 1967, this enchanting tale is about a clockwork toy's quest to become self-winding. Hoban delights in the juxtaposition of supreme silliness and philosophical ideas of Zen-like beauty and simplicity. A most entertaining and soul-satisfying book."

—Jean Matthews, *Chapter One Book Store*, Hamilton, MT

OLIVIA KIDNEY

BY ELLEN POTTER
ILLUSTRATED BY PETER H. REYNOLDS

"Olivia Kidney has a strange life! Especially when she moves into a new apartment building, which is complete with talking lizards, an exiled princess, and an apartment made of glass! Will Olivia's life become any better, or will chaos reign forever? A definite first-rate read about a true first-rate kid."

—Heather Young, *Fireside Bookstore*, Forest City, NC

THE SEQUEL TO OLIVIA KIDNEY:
Olivia Kidney and the Exit Academy

PETER AND THE STARCATCHERS

BY DAVE BARRY AND RIDLEY PEARSON
ILLUSTRATED BY GREG CALL

"Arrr matey! Hop on board this swashbuckling adventure that tells the story of how Peter Pan came to be. A fantastic read-aloud for younger fans of Neverland, too."

—**Sonya Yruel**, *The Storyteller*, Lafayette, CA

SAHARA SPECIAL

BY ESMÉ RAJI CODELL

"Sahara is a gifted writer trapped in a lonely, troubled ten-year-old. A brilliant, compassionate, eccentric teacher and a determined, supportive mom help her unlock her gifts. For fans of Codell's *Educating Esmé*, the news is great: Her previous novel is an exuberant success."

—**Banna Rubinow**, *The River's End Bookstore*, Oswego, NY

SAMMY KEYES & THE HOTEL THIEF
BY WENDELIN VAN DRAANEN
ILLUSTRATED BY DAN YACCANNO

"Sammy Keyes is the modern kid's answer to Nancy Drew. Smart, funny and always in the wrong place at the wrong time, she always manages to save the day."
— **Megan Scott**, *Scott's Bookstore*, Mt. Vernon, WA

ALSO IN THE SAMMY KEYES SERIES:
Sammy Keyes and the Skeleton Man, Sammy Keyes and the Sisters of Mercy, Sammy Keyes and the Runaway Elf, Sammy Keyes and the Curse of Moustache Mary, and more

THE SANDS OF TIME
BY MICHAEL HOEYE

"Another delightful adventure with Hermux Tantamoq, the mouse watchmaker we met in *Time Stops for No Mouse*. He is back with his friends in search of an ancient civilization of mythical creatures called 'cats.' Did these fearsome beasts actually exist? Travel with Hermux through another exciting exploit and find out."
— **Mary Swanson**, *The Bookloft*, Enterprise, OR

ALSO IN THE HERMUX TANTAMOQ TRILOGY:
Time Stops for No Mouse and *No Time Like Show Time*

THE SEA OF TROLLS

*★ BY NANCY FARMER

"Eleven-year-old Jack is apprenticed to the Bard when the berserkers kidnap him and his younger sister (whom they mistake for a princess). This hearty, realistic fantasy will delight kids and adults alike. But be warned: Their adventure kept me up too late for several nights in a row."
—**Jodi Schneider**, *Odyssey Bookshop*, South Hadley, MA

THE SECRETS OF BELLTOWN
A BELLTOWN MYSTERY

*★ BY T.M. MURPHY

"The Belltown books are great favorites of ours. They're on the order of *The Hardy Boys* or *The Three Investigators*. The sleuth is a high school kid, Orville Jacques, who's always finding reasons to investigate long-unsolved cases. But he's sharper than many of the other local characters, and out-gumshoes 'em every time. The stories have made readers of many reluctant eight- to twelve-year-olds."
—**Carol Chittenden**, *Eight Cousins Bookstore*,
Falmouth, MA

ALSO IN A BELLTOWN MYSTERY SERIES:
The Secrets of Cranberry Beach, *The Secrets of Cain's Castle*, *The Secrets of Pilgrim Pond*, *The Secrets of Code Z*, and *The Secrets of the Twisted Cross*

A SERIES OF UNFORTUNATE EVENTS
THE BAD BEGINNING
BY LEMONY SNICKET

"Mr. Snicket faithfully provides exemplary vocabulary lessons, all the while chronicling the misfortunes of the Baudelaire orphans, who, despite misery upon misery heaped upon them by the dim and the vile, persist in their unwavering good-naturedness."
—**Melissa Mytinger**, *Cody's*, Berkeley, CA

ALSO IN A SERIES OF UNFORTUNATE EVENTS:
The Vile Village, The Hostile Hospital, The Carnivorous Carnival, The Slippery Slope, The Grim Grotto, and more

THE STAR OF KAZAN
BY EVA IBBOTSON
ILLUSTRATED BY KEVIN HAWKES

"From the very first page of *The Star of Kazan*, I could imagine myself right alongside of Annika, from her adoption by kindly house servants who find her abandoned on a church doorstep as a baby, to her life in a respectable neighborhood in Vienna under the old Emperor, Franz Joseph. One day, a glamorous stranger appears, and Annika's life is changed forever. This is a wonderful story for young readers and adults alike."
—**Kristine Kaufman**, *The Snow Goose Bookstore*, Stanwood, WA

THE STORY OF THE SEAGULL AND THE CAT WHO TAUGHT HER TO FLY

BY LUIS SEPULVEDA

ILLUSTRATED BY CHRIS SHEBAN

"A comfortable house cat is entrusted with a seagull egg that hatches into a beautiful baby seagull who needs to learn how to fly. This story, filled with charm and hope, will set your heart soaring like a seagull in the wind."

—Deborah Woolsey, *Dragonwings Bookstore*, Waupaca, WI

THE TALE OF DESPEREAUX

BY KATE DiCAMILLO

ILLUSTRATED BY TIMOTHY BASIL ERING

"I'll confess: I've got a thing for books about mice. *The Tale of Despereaux* definitely twitched my whiskers. Kate DiCamillo again proves herself to be a master of narration, creating characters who practically whisper in the ears of her readers, drawing us ever closer to the marvelous worlds of her oh-so-imaginative invention."

—Alison Morris, *Wellesley Booksmith*, Wellesley, MA

THE THIEF LORD
BY CORNELIA FUNKE

"Angels, dragons, and winged lions watch over Venice as six children sneak into houses looking for goods to steal and sell. On the run from a wicked aunt and uncle, they discover the magical powers of an old carousel and what people will do for eternal youth. Full of mischief, adventure, heroes, and magic, this is one of those books that will be read and loved by people of all ages!"

—**Nikki Mutch**, *UConn Co-op*, Storrs, CT

THE TIGER RISING
BY KATE DiCAMILLO
ILLUSTRATED BY CHRIS SHEBAN

"DiCamillo has a way of getting under the skin of her characters with just a few well-chosen words. *The Tiger Rising* brings the reader into a magical story of loss, love and friendship. I'm so glad I came upon this author early in her career so I can read every new book of hers as they come off the press."

—**Fred Powell**, *Main Street Books*, Frostburg, MD

THE TRANSMOGRIFICATION OF ROSCOE WIZZLE

BY DAVID ELLIOTT
ILLUSTRATED BY VLADIMIR RADUNSKY

"A cross between Roald Dahl and Franz Kafka, this
is a fun book about changing, but it also reassures
children that everything really will turn out okay. It is
just the kind of wacky book kids of all ages will gobble
up and laugh over for weeks."
—Katharine Nevins, *Main Street Book Ends*,
Warner, NH

WHALES ON STILTS!
M.T. ANDERSON'S THRILLING TALES

BY M.T. ANDERSON
ILLUSTRATED BY KURT CYRUS

"Whales walk and a strange narrator talks (to you, quirky
reader) in this zany adventure full of evil science and bad
jokes! Join one normal girl and her two wonderfully
clichéd (but loyal) friends on their fast-paced journey of
thrills and chills. Sensationalist and silly, M.T. Anderson's
new adventure tale is sure to entertain readers with a love
of the absurd and a tongue-in-cheek sense of humor."
—Alison Morris, *Wellesley Booksmith*, Wellesley, MA

Children's Book, copyright © 1997 by Peter Sís

YOUNG ADULT

René Kirkpatrick, *All for Kids Books & Music*, Seattle, WA

IN THE WORLD OF LITERATURE, YOUNG-ADULT FICTION IS A relatively new genre. In fact, when I was a kid we went right from middle-grade to adult fiction. It wasn't until Judy Blume penned *Are You There God? It's Me, Margaret* and S. E. Hinton wrote *The Outsiders* that anyone thought to create a teen protagonist. These books remain classics because they deal with issues that were relevant then and are still relevant now. Today, young-adult fiction comes in many forms. It can be funny, poignant, disquieting, or riveting. But nearly all titles have a common denominator: characters with which teens can identify. A few of my favorites: *Cuba 15; Honey, Baby, Sweetheart;* and *A Great and Terrible Beauty.*

There has been much debate about what subject matter is appropriate for teens and, while I believe there are titles that push the edge of appropriateness, there are a number of books that handle sensitive issues well. One of the best books on a controversial subject is Meg Cabot's *Ready or Not,* which is about an almost-17-year-old deciding if she is ready to have sex with her steady boyfriend. Handled with humor and a healthy dose of reality, this book lets the reader think about sex without embarrassment. Like it or not, this stuff happens. I think it's helpful for teens to live vicariously through books. They can process the experience without actually dealing with the consequences.

On the other hand, if a topic hits too close to home, reading about a like-minded protagonist can be emotionally daunting. And that's where I think fantasy books can be a terrific release. *Ender's Game* and *The House of the Scorpion* do an excellent job of tackling difficult subject matter in a non-threatening way. In both stories, the protagonists are forced to find their way in a world where their elders don't have their best interests at heart. But when the action takes place in an alternate universe rather than in a familiar landscape the emotional fallout can be far more palatable.

Still, there's a big difference between what's appropriate for a 12-year-old and what's appropriate for an 18-year-old. Only a parent can decide what's suitable for their child. But unlike movies, books don't come with ratings. As a result, it's not always easy to tell the racy from the reserved. For insight, ask your local bookseller for guidance. He or she is ready and willing to help.

AFTER

BY FRANCINE PROSE

"Francine Prose's first novel for young readers is engaging and timely, and encourages readers to think about freedom and democracy, and whether both are taken for granted."
—**Terry Cox**, *Bohannons' Books With a Past,* Georgetown, KY

ABARAT

BY CLIVE BARKER

"The magic of the Abarat will carry readers away to a land filled with magic, adventure and excitement! Once you start reading this book, you won't want to put it down! I know I can't wait for the next book in the series!"
—**Dennis Bowers**, *Outwrite Bookstore & Coffeehouse,* Atlanta, GA

ALSO IN THE ABARAT SERIES:
Abarat: Days of Magic, Nights of War

THE AMAZING MAURICE AND HIS EDUCATED RODENTS
BY TERRY PRATCHETT

"Pratchett has combined the essential ingredients (great story, great characters, humor, suspense) and crafted a marvelous book."
—Carrie Elizabeth, *Inklings Bookshop*, Yakima, WA

THE AMBER SPYGLASS
BY PHILIP PULLMAN

"This is the magnificent conclusion to a trilogy I never wanted to see end. The writing is masterful; you are there every step of the way. I gasped, I hoped, I cried. Rarely have I read such an exciting adventure that touched on such meaningful topics and resonated so deeply within me. This is not a book just for young adults; I strongly recommend it to anyone who has ever given their faith serious thought. Not to be missed!"
—Elaine Sopchak, *The Book Rack & Children's Pages*, *Champlain Mill*, Winooski, VT

ALSO IN HIS DARK MATERIALS TRILOGY:
The Golden Compass and *The Subtle Knife*

ANGUS, THONGS AND FULL-FRONTAL SNOGGING
CONFESSIONS OF GEORGIA NICOLSON
BY LOUISE RENNISON

"This is a hilarious, and brazenly honest, account of the very complicated world that is the life of a fourteen-year-old London girl."
—**Danielle Morgan**, *Village Books*, Bellingham, WA

ALSO IN THE CONFESSIONS OF GEORGIA NICOLSON SERIES:
On the Bright Side, I'm Now the Girlfriend of a Sex God; Knocked Out by My Nunga-Nunga's; Away Laughing on a Fast Camel; and more

ARTEMIS FOWL
BY EOIN COLFER

"A twelve-year-old villain kidnaps a fairy in order to get the fairy gold, but these trolls and gnomes are not the ones from fairy tales; they are armed and dangerous with the most amazing up-to-date gadgets. I just loved the language and vocabulary, and that the author never talks down to kids. An action-packed fantasy."
—**Sue Boucher**, *Lake Forest Book Store*, Lake Forest, IL

ALSO IN THE ARTEMIS FOWL SERIES:
The Arctic Incident, The Eternity Code, and *The Opal Deception*

BLOOD RED HORSE
BOOK ONE OF THE
DE GRANVILLE TRILOGY
BY K. M. GRANT

"Set during the Crusades, this story features an
extraordinary horse named Hosanna. William, a young
knight serving King Richard, and Kamil, a Muslim serving
Saladin, find in their shared love for the mortally wounded
Hosanna the will to pray together to God, Allah, Christ,
and Mohammed. In this story, young people will glimpse
the possibilities of healing on many levels."

—**Janet Owens**, *Millrace Books*, Farmington, CT

BLOODY JACK
BEING AN ACCOUNT OF THE
CURIOUS ADVENTURES OF MARY
"JACKY" FABER, SHIP'S BOY
BY L.A. MEYER

"Jacky Faber is a thirteen-year-old with spirit and grit.
She's an orphan living on the streets of eighteenth-century
London, begging for food and dodging danger. When a
warship comes to shore looking for ship's boys, Jacky
disguises herself as a boy and sets out on a high sea
adventure in search of pirates. This one will keep
you reading!"

—**Valerie Lewis**, *Hicklebee's*, San Jose, CA

BROKEN HEARTS... HEALING
YOUNG POETS SPEAK OUT ON DIVORCE
EDITED BY TOM WORTHEN, PH.D.

"Wonderful poetry written by children to show their real feelings on the subject of divorce. It is great for children to help them deal with divorce and for adults to help them understand how their children may be feeling."
— **Sam Canaday**, *Brace Books & More*, Ponca City, OK

CITY OF THE BEASTS
BY ISABEL ALLENDE

"For the young and the young at heart, this story about the relationship between a nerdy boy and his adventurous grandmother is priceless. The adventure story has just enough magic to make it thought-provoking fiction, but not so much to make it a flat-out fantasy. A wonderful book."
— **Jeanne Michael**, *Odyssey Books*, Grass Valley, CA

ERAGON
INHERITANCE, BOOK I
BY CHRISTOPHER PAOLINI

"*Eragon* is a guaranteed hit for any reader who loves fantasy. Drawing on the tradition of J.R.R. Tolkien, Anne McCaffrey, Ursula K. Le Guin, Philip Pullman, and other great fantasists, Christopher Paolini has woven together an exciting suspense-filled adventure of one young man coming of age in partnership with the first dragon born in over a century. I can't wait to read the rest of the trilogy."
—**Peter Glassman**, *Books of Wonder,* New York, NY

ALSO IN THE INHERITANCE TRILOGY: *Eldest*

GEOGRAPHY CLUB
BY BRENT HARTINGER

"Dealing with the hopes, and, yes, even desires of gay teenagers is bound to make this book controversial, but those who read it will be rewarded with an honest portrayal of the downside to high school popularity and the peer pressure, which can lead kids into taunting other kids. The author uses great characters and humor to tackle a difficult subject and, in the end, gives us a glimpse at the injuries caused by intolerance and the importance of standing up for society's outcasts."
—**Vincent Desjardins**, *The Snow Goose Bookstore,* Stanwood, WA

GIFTS

BY URSULA K. LE GUIN

"This is a rare and intelligent teen fantasy from the acclaimed author of the *Earthsea Cycle*. Orrec and Gry live in a world where family and lands are guarded fiercely with dark and powerful gifts—the ability to twist limbs, to blind and deafen, to enslave minds—but they find the courage to throw off their families' expectations and envision a world of light and grace. Highly recommended."
—**Kim Fox**, *Schuler Books & Music*, Grand Rapids, MI

GINGERBREAD

BY RACHEL COHN

"This is a sharply funny and refreshingly angst-free book, with the most electric female protagonist I've ever found in young adult fiction. Cohn has such a spectacularly unique voice that by the end of the first paragraph, one realizes it is something energetic and special. What a great summertime read!"
—**Carla Jeffries**, *Harry W. Schwartz Bookshop*, Shorewood, WI

THE GOLEM'S EYE
THE BARTIMAEUS TRILOGY, BOOK 2
BY JONATHAN STROUD

"Bartimaeus and Nathaniel are back! It's two years later, magicians still rule London, and Nathaniel has been promoted to a position in internal affairs, working to fight The Resistance. With action, magic, and fabulous character development, Stroud lives up to the expectations of his *Amulet of Samarkand (Book 1)* fans!"
    —**McKenna Jordan**, *Murder by the Book*, Houston, TX

ALSO IN THE BARTIMAEUS TRILOGY:
Amulet of Samarkand and *Ptolemy's Gate*

A HAT FULL OF SKY
BY TERRY PRATCHETT

"Pratchett has outdone himself in this sequel to *The Wee Free Men*, which sees an older Tiffany going to the mountains to learn more about witchcraft. It is full of fun, but, like all great literature, the book is multilayered and examines seriously (as well as humorously) what it means to be human and what those gifted with special talents owe to the rest of humanity."
    —**Charlene Taylor**, *Reader's Oasis*, Tucson, AZ

HOLD FAST

BY KEVIN MAJOR

"This is a Canadian coming-of-age story told in the first
person and spoken from the heart with disarming honesty.
When Michael's parents are killed in a car crash, his life
is changed in an instant. He must leave his small
Newfoundland outpost community to live with his aunt
and uncle in St. Albert, where he is faced with rigidity and
verbal abuse. The recognition of his hurt and his need to
be independent moves the action to a swift, sometimes
edgy, and finally redemptive conclusion."

—Janet Clymer, *The Toadstool Bookshop*, Keene, NH

HONEY, BABY, SWEETHEART

BY DEB CALETTI

"A wise, witty, and hilarious story that looks at coming-
of-age and so much more. This multigenerational love story
is extremely well-written and should appeal both
to teenagers and adults. I couldn't stop nodding and
laughing in thorough understanding!"

—Morgan Spring, *Full Circle Bookstore*,
Oklahoma City, OK

IN THE SHADOW OF THE ARK

BY ANNE PROVOOST

"Re Jana's family has fled home for the desert, for dryer land. Noah and his three sons are building an ark, but no one believes that the predicted floods will come. The story of what ensues is a literary page-turner and a great love story."

—**Barb MacDonald**, *Great Northern Books and Hobbies,*
Oscoda, MI

INDIGO

BY ALICE HOFFMAN

"Oak Grove is a dry and dusty place, and everyone who lives there likes it that way, except the McGill brothers. They prefer anchovy pie to blueberry, pour salt into their water, and have faint blue webbing between their fingers and toes. Like Hoffman's previous novel *Aquamarine*, this is a mysterious and magical tale that will delight its readers."

—**Mary Kooyman**, *Scott's Bookstore,* Mount Vernon, WA

KIT'S WILDERNESS

BY DAVID ALMOND

"In this story, Kit follows his troubled friend, David, down a dark road into their ancestral past. With the strength of his family's love, and the guidance of his grandfather's stories, Kit is able to help David find the goodness and compassion that resides within; an exceptional book for young adults that is not to be missed."
—**Judy Hobbs**, *Third Place Books*, Lake Forest Park, WA

THE LIGHTKEEPER'S DAUGHTER

BY IAIN LAWRENCE

"This intense family drama plays itself out through flashbacks that solve the mystery of how the lighthouse keeper's daughter became pregnant and how her brother died. Written in beautiful prose and astonishingly precise metaphors that help the reader see and feel what the characters experience, the book explores deep psychological themes related to the family that are at once biblical, Freudian, and utopian. The book is pure reading pleasure! What a superb author."
—**Betty Renner**, *Merritt Bookshops,* Millbrook, NY

MESSENGER
BY LOIS LOWRY

"Lois Lowry has done it again! This novel is perfection.
Bits of *The Giver* and *Gathering Blue* are woven into a
stunning book. How brilliantly she incorporates the
values of acceptance, caring, and respect into a novel."
— **Susan Capaldi**, *McLean & Eakin Booksellers*,
Petoskey, MI

MONTMORENCY ON THE ROCKS
BY ELEANOR UPDALE

"What a pleasure to see the return of Montmorency, the thief
turned aristocrat! As Montmorency struggles with opium
addiction, he's called upon to solve a series of bombings in
London. What follows is a mystery that will take him and his
cohorts to the rural island of Tarimond and back, where they
find more questions before they find answers."
— **Sarah Todd**, *Children's Book World*, Haverford, PA

ALSO IN THE MONTMORENCY SERIES:
Montmorency: Thief, Liar, Gentleman

A NORTHERN LIGHT

BY JENNIFER DONNELLY

"This amazing novel chronicles the life of Mathilda in upstate New York, in alternating times of early spring and late summer. She is torn between going to college and keeping her promise to her dying mother to stay and take care of the family. This is absolutely the best book I have read in years."

—**Heather M. Fierst**, *The Book Bag*, Valparaiso, IN

PLACES I NEVER MEANT TO BE
Original Stories by Censored Writers

EDITED BY JUDY BLUME

"A superb collection by some of the best YA authors writing today. A bonus is a short essay by each author on the topic of censorship."

—**Judy Park**, *Mostly Books*, Gig Harbor, WA

PLEASE DON'T KILL THE FRESHMAN
A MEMOIR
BY ZOE TROPE

"This collection of journal entries from author Zoe Trope's first two years of high school is a refreshingly honest alternative to the run-of-the-mill adolescent novels. Her introspective and engaging writing draws the reader into the everyday thoughts and actions of a truly exceptional and talented teenage girl."

—**Samantha Pitchell**, *Newtonville Books*, Newton, MA

THE SAME STUFF AS STARS
BY KATHERINE PATERSON

"Angel and her brother are deserted by their mother, so they are left in the care of their great grandmother, who is very poor. Angel, who is eleven, has to be adult and parent, too; her burdens seem positively overwhelming. But she manages to find some joy in life as she discovers the stars with the help of an elderly man in the trailer next door. A very compelling story."

—**Kim Dalley**, *Toadstool Books*, Peterborough, NH

SANG SPELL

BY PHYLLIS REYNOLDS NAYLOR

"A teenage boy is robbed and beaten while hitchhiking,
and regains consciousness in what seems to be another
time and place. Not an ordinary time travel story, this
strange and mysterious tale of the boy's efforts to figure
out where he is and how he can get home is gripping
and intriguing."
   —**Harvada Elisberg**, *Children's Bookshop*, Appleton, WI

THE SEEING STONE

BY KEVIN CROSSLEY-HOLLAND

"While many writers have tried their hands at the
Arthurian saga, this author has truly brought it to life.
He combines humor, rich prose and scholarship with
characters you care about. Here is the first in a trilogy that
will, like Harry Potter, be enjoyed by readers of all ages."
   —**Rita Moran**, *Apple Valley Books*, Winthrop, ME

ALSO IN THE ARTHUR TRILOGY:
At the Crossing Places and *King of the Middle March*

SHADOWMANCER

BY G.P. TAYLOR

"This story of mythology, history, folklore, magic, and smuggling is tightly woven into a totally terrific tale of good versus evil. First-time author Taylor spins a plot so intense it will leave your imagination tingling!"

—**Deborah Woolsey**, *Dragonwings Bookstore*, Waupaca, WI

SHATTERING GLASS

BY GAIL GILES

"From the first sentence ('Simon Glass was easy to hate') to the violent ending, this is a provocative novel on the nature of leaders and followers, the price of being cool, and the pain of wanting to belong in high school. Dark and well crafted, this suspenseful and powerful book is unforgettable, and it will provoke much discussion."

—**Holly Myers**, *Elliott Bay Book Company*, Seattle, WA

SHOOTER

BY WALTER DEAN MYERS

"The book eases the reader into a Columbine-like story, as the details of the 'incident' and the prior weeks are revealed via several interviews, reports, newspaper articles, and a diary. This is likely to be a disturbing book for many; however, it has the potential to open a dialogue between students and adults alike."

—**Gwen Harding-Peets**, *Merritt Books*, Millbrook, NY

THE SILENT BOY

BY LOIS LOWRY

"Perfection. That is the one word I would use to describe this tale of a young doctor's daughter and a 'touched boy,' who doesn't speak to humans but relates to animals and mimics their noises. Haunting and beautiful, this book should be a staple of everyone's library, right next to *Number the Stars* and *The Giver*."

—**Nikki Mutch**, *UConn Co-op*, Storrs, CT

THE SISTERHOOD OF THE TRAVELING PANTS

BY ANN BRASHARES

"This is a wonderful read for young women. The characters struggle with boyfriends, death, families, first jobs and a summer away from each other. But they survive it all with the help of a special pair of jeans."

—**Aubrey S. Davis**, *Arches Book Company,* Moab, UT

ALSO IN THE SISTERHOOD OF THE TRAVELING PANTS SERIES: *The Second Summer of the Sisterhood* and *Girls In Pants: The Third Summer of the Sisterhood*

THE SLEDDING HILL

BY CHRIS CRUTCHER

"As it details the life history of a banned book from a teenager's perspective, *The Sledding Hill* is a brilliant chronicle about censorship in literature and its effect on personal freedom. But this book speaks to my heart because it's a story about undying friendship and the vast capacity for reasoning in the most unreasonable kids."

—**Collette Morgan**, *Wild Rumpus,* Minneapolis, MN

THE SLIGHTLY TRUE STORY OF CEDAR B. HARTLEY
(WHO PLANNED TO LIVE AN UNUSUAL LIFE)
BY MARTINE MURRAY

"A wonderful story of a girl walking the tightrope between childhood and adolescence. Cedar is a remarkable twelve-year-old who is able to maintain the confidence that makes young children so admirable while accepting the wisdom that comes with growing up."

—**Kyla Hilton**, *Taylor Books*, Charleston, WV

SO B. IT
BY SARAH WEEKS

"Heidi, her mentally disabled mother, Sophie, and their neighbor Bernadette live a pretty unusual life. Heidi's mother knows twenty-three words and Bernadette is agoraphobic. Together, the three of them are a family, caring for each other, until the year Heidi turns twelve and begins to wonder about who her father was. Unable to get any information, she decides to try to find out on her own. This is a beautifully written book about family and love and knowing what is really important."

—**René Kirkpatrick**, *All for Kids Books & Music*, Seattle, WA

STARGIRL

BY JERRY SPINELLI

"The students at Mica High have no idea what to make of Stargirl, a tenth-grader who plays the ukulele, keeps a pet rat in her bag, and dances in the rain. This story of individuality, conformity, peer pressure, and first love touched me deeply with its truth and beauty. I paused for a few days before I finished because I didn't want to say good-bye to Stargirl. I found I didn't have to."

—**Mari Enoch**, *The Bookloft*, Great Barrington, MA

TANGLED THREADS
A HMONG GIRL'S STORY

BY PEGI DEITZ SHEA

"After ten years in a Thai refugee camp, a Laotian girl and her grandmother (whom we first met in the author's *The Whispering Cloth*) have realized their dream of joining their relatives in America. Pegi Deitz Shea describes the fascinating Hmong culture as she sensitively and realistically portrays the dilemmas both generations face as they struggle to adjust to life in America."

—**Janet Owens**, *Millrace Books*, Farmington, CT

VOTE FOR LARRY

BY JANET TASHJIAN

"I really liked Tashjian's *The Gospel According to Larry*, but I loved, loved, loved *Vote for Larry*! This story of an unlikely campaign makes an excellent jumping-off point for political discussions, and it should be read by everyone, adults as well as teens."

—Merrilee Wilkerson, *BookPeople*, Austin, TX

THE WHALE RIDER

BY WITI IHIMAERA

"In this wonderfully inspiring story, the focus is a spirited young girl, Kahu, and her curmudgeonly great-grandfather, the chief of a Maori tribe and the descendant of the ancient whale rider. Kahu's tribe is in danger of losing its identity unless a descendant carries on the sacred traditions for the village. The old chief is convinced the true heir must be a boy and sees no use for Kahu. However, she has inherited the sacred gift from the whale rider and must convince her great-grandfather she can save the tribe. This story of faith and tenacity for children and adults is sure to become a classic."

—Bunny Thompson, *Paulina Springs Book Company*,
Sisters, OR

WITCH CHILD

BY CELIA REES

"Through the journal of Mary Newbery, the story of her grandmother's death by hanging for witchcraft unfolds. Mary finds passage to America in 1659, where she becomes part of an inflexible Puritan community. Her desire to belong, resistance to conform, and eventual self-acceptance will provide teens with a truly heroic model to emulate."

—**Kathy Carrigan**, *Harry W. Schwartz Bookshops*, Milwaukee, WI

WITNESS

BY KAREN HESSE

"A remarkable book, written in poetic form using eleven different voices, telling of the effect of the Ku Klux Klan on a 1924 Vermont community. Suspenseful, scary, yet often funny and thrilling, it is the saga of ordinary people in extraordinary circumstances. How they then react and survive is both tragic and heroic. A wonderful new novel from Hesse."

—**Marge Grutzmacher**, *Passtimes Books*, Sister Bay, WI

NONFICTION

Alison Morris, *Wellesley Booksmith*, Wellesley, MA

WHEN I WAS ABOUT SEVEN YEARS OLD, MY MOTHER unearthed a box of her favorite childhood books and passed them along to me. I recall parting their worn covers and seeing her name penned on the title page in charmingly childish script—powerful evidence that she too had been a child once (and a reader, at that).

Seeing her name in those books infused my reading with a wonderful sense of history repeating itself. And perhaps this connection to history was what guided my preferences, as the ones I loved most were biographies—several volumes from the *Childhood of Famous Americans* series first published in the early 1940s. I devoured them, savoring the early adventures of Amelia Earhart, Ben Franklin, Juliette Gordon Low, Daniel Boone, and Kit Carson.

I had been taught in school that the definition of nonfiction was "true stories," and to me this meant "full of facts" about real people, real things, real events. I now believe, though, that what made these stories "true" was not so much the facts they contained, but the truths I gleaned from them. In the case of those *Childhood of Famous Americans* books, the truth I learned was that all adults (even the famous ones) have made mistakes, overcome hardships, and once been young and dreaming.

If you ask me, it's this blend of both meaningful truths and interesting facts that makes good nonfiction such a pleasure to read and such a valuable asset to readers of all ages: books that engage the heart and the mind in equal measure are powerful tools. As evidence, take the fact that in recent years I have become passionate about topics that previously held little or no interest for me, as a direct result of reading children's or young adult nonfiction. *The Race to Save the Lord God Bird*, by Phillip Hoose, fueled a new-found obsession with woodpeckers. *This Land Was Made for You and Me: The Life and Songs of Woody Guthrie*, by Elizabeth Partridge, permanently altered the contents of my music collection. *Chuck Close: Up Close*, by Jan Greenberg and Sandra Jordan, fueled a new interest in contemporary painters. And, well...I could go on.

Many of the books you'll find reviewed in this section are books that have introduced me to topics that, it's true, I've become rather passionate about. I have personally read and loved them for both the information they provide and the truths they contain. Hopefully you and your children will, too.

Exchange of the Idea, copyright © 1997 by Peter Sís

PICTURE BOOKS

ACTUAL SIZE

BY STEVE JENKINS

"Jenkins' cut-and-torn paper collages illustrate amazing creatures. The four-inch-long teeth of the great white shark zigzag across two pages, and, in contrast, the dwarf goby—smallest of all fish—could ride on the tip of a thumbnail. An intriguing book for youngsters pondering the wonders of 'big and little.'"

—Jody Fickes Shapiro, *Adventures for Kids,*
Ventura, CA

THE COIN COUNTING BOOK

BY ROZANNE LANCZAK WILLIAMS

"Teachers and parents alike will delight in working with children using this colorful, easy math book. The concepts of spending and saving open doors for fun, discussion, and learning."

—Judy Purdy Fountain, *Ecola Square Books,*
Cannon Beach, OR

FIREBOAT
THE HEROIC ADVENTURES
OF THE JOHN J. HARVEY
WRITTEN AND ILLUSTRATED
BY MAIRA KALMAN

"This is a classic that will be just as powerful fifty years
from now. I am immensely grateful Kalman had this
book in her. Portions of the proceeds of sales of this book
have been donated to the Twin Towers Orphan Fund."
—Tony Miksak,
Gallery Bookshop & Bookwinkle's Children's Books,
Mendocino, CA

LET'S MAKE IT POP-UP
BY DAVID A. CARTER
ILLUSTRATED BY JAMES DIAZ

"What a wonderful way to spend the day
with your children—making pop-up things
for a storybook! This educational and fun book features
bright illustrations and wonderful instructions."
—**Lee Musgjerd,** *Lee's Book Emporium,* Glasgow, MT

ROOTS SHOOTS BUCKETS & BOOTS
Gardening Together with Children
BY SHARON LOVEJOY

"One of the best books about gardens that I've ever seen. Learn how to plant a child's name in lettuce, design a maze of flowers, grow a giant's teepee, and listen to tomatoes gurgle with a stethoscope. Lovejoy has ideas for turning anyone's garden into an educational playground full of wonder and fun."
　　　　—Ellen Davis, *Dragonwings Bookstore*, Waupaca, WI

THE TRAIN OF STATES
BY PETER SÍS

"There's a circus train coming like you've never seen before—each fabulous car showcasing one of the fifty states in glorious detail. I fell in love with this tribute to the United States and to our wonderful tradition of circus trains."
　　　　—Ellen Davis, *Dragonwings Bookstore*, Waupaca, WI

MIDDLE GRADE

BOREDOM BLASTERS
BRAIN BOGGLERS, AWESOME ACTIVITIES, COOL COMICS, TASTY TREATS, AND MORE...
BY HELAINE BECKER
ILLUSTRATED BY CLAUDIA DÁVILA

"This is a flashy, eye-catching book packed with puzzles, jokes, trivia, and creative activity ideas for kids of all ages. Turn off the TV and tune into *Boredom Blasters!*"
—**Cathleen Zehms,** *Dave's Book Center,*
Green Bay, WI

FOLLOW THE TRAIL
A YOUNG PERSON'S GUIDE TO THE GREAT OUTDOORS
BY JESSICA LOY

"This is a great beginners' guide to the outdoors for young children. It touches on everything you might do while camping, from planning the trip to lying under the stars at night. Included are plant and animal identification and good safety tips."
—**Kim Soyka,** *Book House of Stuyvesant Plaza,*
Albany, NY

GIRLS THINK OF EVERYTHING
STORIES OF INGENIOUS INVENTIONS BY WOMEN
BY CATHERINE THIMMESH
ILLUSTRATED BY MELISSA SWEET

"This book is a necessary collection of the stories of the women who invented the Snugli, Liquid Paper, and more. Their creations are some of the most enduring (the windshield wiper) and the most loved (the chocolate-chip cookie). Thimmesh thoroughly researched each inventor's story and, when possible, interviewed each. The book is complemented by Sweet's wacky collages."

—**Amanda Himle**, *The Red Balloon Bookshop,*
St. Paul, MN

KIDCHAT
QUESTIONS TO FUEL YOUNG MINDS AND MOUTHS
BY BRET NICHOLAUS AND PAUL LOWRIE

"This is a great book for both parents and teachers, full of thought-provoking questions that will start a good dialog between adult and child."

—**Rita Moran**, *Apple Valley Books,*
Winthrop, ME

MATH-TERPIECES
The Art of Problem-Solving
BY GREG TANG
ILLUSTRATED BY GREG PAPROCKI

"Experience the artwork of twelve great masters while solving math problems. Tang has once again made math fun by combining it with an artist familiar to most children. Each work is accompanied by a poem challenging the reader to group representative objects on the opposite page. An entertaining extension to a math curriculum."

—**Julie Gaston**, *Butterfly Books*, De Pere, WI

Q IS FOR QUARK
A Science Alphabet Book
BY DAVID M. SCHWARTZ
ILLUSTRATED BY KIM DONER

"Excellent illustrations and an informative text make complex concepts easy to understand. We give this book a very high rating."

—**Bob Spear**, *The Book Barn*, Leavenworth, KS

RIDER IN THE SKY
How an American Cowboy Built England's First Airplane
BY JOHN R. HULLS
ILLUSTRATED BY DAVID WEITZMAN

"Hulls explores the fascinating life story of Samuel Cody, an American cowboy who went from performing in a Wild West show, to building gigantic kites and experimenting with gliders, to, finally, building Britain's first airplane in 1908. Filled with dozens of period photographs and illustrations, this book is a well-written account of a little-known aviation pioneer."

—**Allan Kausch**, *Copperfield's Books,* Petaluma, CA

SHIPWRECKED!
The True Adventures of a Japanese Boy
BY RHODA BLUMBERG

"We follow the life of a fourteen-year-old castaway who becomes the first Japanese person to enter the U.S. and later becomes an honored samurai. The gripping text sheds light on a variety of historical topics; this is inspiring, fast-paced adventure."

—**Jane Baldus**, *Anderson's Bookshop,* Naperville, IL

SHOW; DON'T TELL!
SECRETS OF WRITING
BY JOSEPHINE NOBISSO
ILLUSTRATED BY EVA MONTANARI

"This is a wonderfully illustrated book that is actually a lesson in how to write a story. There are tactile pieces, a scratch-and-sniff section, and a sound chip. Nobisso's story is a wonderful lesson, and Montanari's drawings are charming and funny."
—Terry Lucas, *The Open Book,* Westhampton Beach, NY

YOUNG ADULT

ALONE ACROSS THE ARCTIC
ONE WOMAN'S EPIC JOURNEY BY DOG TEAM
BY PAM FLOWERS WITH ANN DIXON

"Flowers is the tremendous human being who completed this journey with her dogsled team, meeting many perils along the way. What a fascinating and fulfilling read; I am still in awe of this courageous journey!"
—Dana Harper, *Brystone Children's Books,* Watauga, TX

GIRLOSOPHY
A SOUL SURVIVAL KIT
❧ BY ANTHEA PAUL

"This is the book for any young woman going through anything traumatic, from breaking up to changing schools. It is a sampler for life filled with no-nonsense sayings and articles on being true to yourself, without being sentimental or sweet. Many young women I have given this to have said it has changed their lives."

——**René Kirkpatrick**, *All for Kids Books and Music*,
Seattle, WA

ALSO IN THE GIRLOSOPHY SERIES:
Girlosophy: The Breakup Survival Guide, Girlosophy: Real Girls' Stories, and more

HARLEM STOMP!
A CULTURAL HISTORY OF
THE HARLEM RENAISSANCE
❧ BY LABAN CARRICK HILL

"*Harlem Stomp!* leaves no element of the Harlem Renaissance untouched. As gorgeous as it is informative, the poems, paintings, and sculptures of great writers and artists cascade across each page, buoyed by Hill's spirited, detailed writing."

——**Beth Isaacson**, *Politics and Prose Books & Coffeehouse*,
Washington, DC

HOLE IN MY LIFE
❧ BY JACK GANTOS

"Gantos has written a courageous and compelling
autobiographical book about his time as a drug smuggler.
The consequences were awful: He was caught, convicted,
and served fifteen harrowing months in prison. Gantos has
not only written a good book, but also, I hope, has opened
the possibility of writing about far wider motives for
decisions and actions that sculpt lives into their actual
form. Living with today's pervasive drug culture is an
unsought challenge each person is forced to face. A very
important book."

—Carol Chittenden, *Eight Cousins Bookshop,*
Falmouth, MA

IN MY HANDS
MEMORIES OF A
HOLOCAUST RESCUER
❧ BY IRENE GUT OPDYKE
WITH JENNIFER ARMSTRONG

"I've been telling everyone about this powerful book
about a young, inspiring heroine. Now that it's in
paperback, it's perfect for school reading lists as well as
adult reading groups. Please read it!"

—Betsey Detwiler, *Buttonwood Books and Toys,*
Cohasset, MA

OF BEETLES AND ANGELS
A Boy's Remarkable Journey
from a Refugee Camp to Harvard
BY MAWI ASGEDOM

"Asgedom gives eloquent voice to his Ethiopian family and their new life in America. Living in poverty and confronting racism, he still looks for and finds beauty in other people. An inspiring true story."
  —Linda Ramsdell, *The Galaxy Bookshop*, Hardwick, VT

SHADOW LIFE
A Portrait of Anne Frank
and Her Family
BY BARRY DENENBERG

"As I read *Shadow Life*, I found I could hardly put it down. I learned more about what the Franks ate, what they read, how they lived, and, always, the fear that was part of it all. This is a title I'll enthusiastically sell in my store."
                    —Dorothy Dickerson, *Books & More*,
                                        Albion, MI

HOLIDAY

Ellen Davis, *President of the Association of Booksellers for*
Children, Dragonwings Bookstore, Waupaca, WI

EVERYONE CELEBRATES. AROUND THE WORLD AND IN
America, which holds the diversity of the world within its
borders, traditions and holidays may be different from
family to family, region to region, and culture to culture—but all of us have traditions and holidays, and we
all have celebrations.

A tradition may be a small celebration of a familiar
moment in the pattern of time, and perhaps when a group
of traditions are celebrated all at once it becomes a holiday.
In every culture the holidays celebrated throughout a year
mark the passage of the seasons. It could be that the desire
to celebrate the seasons is one of humanity's deepest common bonds.

In this age of screens and schedules, we sometimes lose
touch with our connection to the natural world. Celebrating
the seasons can help reassure children of their place in the
passage of time and in the big world. They become aware of
how their small, daily rhythms fit into the larger rhythms of
life. The holidays of each season are an occasion for stories
of the past to take center stage, and as children grow and the

cycle of holidays are repeated, new memories are made, and a new generation finds a home in the family stories.

When choosing books for holidays, many families will look for history, religion, diversity, or nostalgia. Wonderful books on these topics will be easy to find displayed on bookstore shelves decorated with Santas, turkeys, and hearts, but remember to also delve a little deeper. Look for those books that celebrate the seasons, stories that you can dip into throughout the year. Maybe you will create a new tradition of reading *The Snowy Day* when the first snow falls, chapters of *The Long Winter* on January nights, *Blueberries for Sal* at your first summer picnic, and chapters of *A Long Way from Chicago* on summer evenings. Perhaps on special nights every month you will go through the seasons with Omakayas in *The Birchbark House*, Almanzo in *Farmer Boy*, Toad in *The Wind in the Willows*, or Grandma Dowdel in *A Year Down Yonder*.

Books read each season with children can become their touchstones for celebrations that will continue to offer a connection to the natural rhythms that we all share.

VALENTINE'S DAY

THE BALLAD OF VALENTINE
BY ALISON JACKSON
ILLUSTRATED BY TRICIA TUSA

Picture Book

"Neither mailman, nor homing pigeon, nor smoke signal can communicate the affections of one shy suitor to his darling Valentine! Will she ever get the message? With this delightful adaptation of the song 'Clementine,' Alison Jackson and Tricia Tusa deliver a Valentine that will warm hearts of all ages and leave readers laughing!"

—**Alison Morris**, *Wellesley Booksmith*, Wellesley, MA

CLIFFORD'S VALENTINES
BY NORMAN BRIDWELL

Early Reader

"Everyone loves Clifford, so, with the cooperation of Mother Nature, Clifford thinks of a clever way to wish everyone Happy Valentine's Day in this charming level-one early reader."

—**Susan Fruncillo**, *Lake Country Booksellers*, White Bear Lake, MN

THWONK
BY JOAN BAUER

Young Adult
"This is a delightfully funny romance novel for teen readers about the dangers of getting what you wish for—in this case a personal Cupid (who, for my money, would look just like Nathan Lane). Yes, young romance can be fun."

—Lanetta W. Parks, *The Compleat Bookseller,*
Chestertown, MD

EASTER

THE COUNTRY BUNNY AND THE LITTLE GOLD SHOES
BY DU BOSE HEYWARD
ILLUSTRATED BY MARJORIE FLACK

Picture Book
"I never grow tried of the lessons Grandfather Bunny and Little Cottontail tell. The rewards of being wise, kind, swift, and brave can come to anyone regardless of size, speed, or wealth."

—Barbara Theroux, *Fact & Fiction,*
Missoula, MT

THE EASTER STORY
 BY GENNADY SPIRIN

Picture Book

"This book remains one of my Easter favorites. The illustrations, full of religious detail, are positively breathtaking. *The Easter Story*, which depicts the events leading up to and following the Crucifixion, can be shared with the whole family."

—**Kimberly Hughes**, *Village Bookstore,* Menomonee Falls, WI

THE GOLDEN EGG BOOK
 BY MARGARET WISE BROWN
ILLUSTRATED BY LEONARD WEISGARD

Babies and Toddlers

"Margaret Wise Brown tells the story of a bunny who learns that an egg won't hatch 'til it's ready. This classic story is as bright and sweet and wholesome as a child's Easter should be, and it's charmingly illustrated by Leonard Weisgard."

—**Laura Huemer**, *Goldfinch Books,* Maplewood, NJ

HOW DO YOU KNOW IT'S EASTER?

BY DIAN CURTIS REGAN

ILLUSTRATED BY FUMI KOSAKA

Babies and Toddlers

"We like to give this book as a welcome alternative to candy in the basket for a little one. You can also read it for a quick snuggle up with mom as the days count down. The lift-the-flaps make it all the more enticing for the toddler set."

—Valerie Koehler, *Blue Willow Bookshop*, Houston, TX

MAX'S CHOCOLATE CHICKEN

BY ROSEMARY WELLS

Babies and Toddlers

"This is a cute Easter book. Max and his sister, Ruby, go on an egg hunt, and the one who finds the most eggs wins the prize—a chocolate chicken. Will Max be able to find more eggs than his sister and win the prize?"

—Leslie Christman, *Horton's Books & Gifts*, Carrollton, GA

RECHENKA'S EGGS
BY PATRICIA POLACCO

Picture Book

"This is a story with glorious artwork, an injured goose, an old woman with a special talent, broken eggs, sorrow, and redemption. Master storyteller Polacco spins a classic tale in an exotic Ukrainian setting, and her warm illustrations never fail to touch our hearts."
—**Ellen Davis**, *Dragonwings Bookstore,* Waupaca, WI

THE TALE OF THREE TREES
BY ANGELA ELWELL HUNT
ILLUSTRATED BY TIM JONKE

Picture Book

"A simple retelling of an old folktale of three trees destined for great things, this story can be read at any time of year. At Easter and during Lent, the story of Christ's sacrifice is accessible to all ages. It's a wonderful baptism/christening gift."
—**Valerie Koehler**, *Blue Willow Bookshop,* Houston, TX

PASSOVER

MIRIAM'S CUP
A PASSOVER STORY
BY FRAN MANUSHKIN
ILLUSTRATED BY BOB DACEY

Picture Book

"This is a beautifully illustrated children's book that tells the story of Miriam, sister of Moses, and of her courage and faith. In this retelling of the Passover story, the role of Miriam is emphasized, as is the joyful nature of the celebration."

—Terry Lucas, *The Open Book*,
Westhampton Beach, NY

A PICKLES PASSOVER
BY RICHIE CHEVAT

Early Reader

"Thanks to Tommy, Angelica, and the rest of the Rugrats gang, my son has been exposed, in a warm and winsome manner, to many traditional holidays not celebrated by our family."

—Maryelizabeth Hart, *Mysterious Galaxy Books*,
San Diego, CA

THE SECRET SEDER

BY DOREEN RAPPAPORT
ILLUSTRATED BY EMILY ARNOLD McCULLY

Picture Book

"Written from the point of view of a French boy whose family is forced to hide their Jewish faith, the story pays tribute to bravery and the proud celebration of religious tradition in the face of horrific acts of genocide. Well-written and featuring beautiful illustrations, this book is terrific."

—Jan Loveland, *Cranesbill Books*, Chelsea, MI

WONDERS AND MIRACLES
A Passover Companion

BY ERIC A. KIMMEL

Middle Grade

"This beautiful companion to the Passover Seder is illustrated with art from 3,000 years of Jewish history. Award-winning author Eric Kimmel gives us stories, songs, poems, prayers, and commentary that will make any Passover Seder more lively and informative for the whole family."

—Mark Brumberg, *National Yiddish Book Center,* Amherst, MA

HALLOWEEN

BAT JAMBOREE
BY KATHI APPELT
ILLUSTRATED BY MELISSA SWEET

Picture Book

"The best Halloween party ever—bats come from all over to celebrate and have fun. The party goes on and on and on, but it isn't over 'til the Bat Lady sings."

—**Dinah Price,** *The Red Balloon,*
San Antonio, TX

A RATTLE OF BONES
A HALLOWEEN BOOK OF COLLECTIVE NOUNS
BY KIPLING WEST

Picture Book

"This is *An Exaltation of Larks* with a Halloween theme. From 'an unkindness of ravens' to a 'murder of crows,' this is a delightful trip through the English language."

—**Shirley Masengill,** *Cover to Cover Booksellers,*
San Francisco, CA

THE SPIDER AND THE FLY

BY MARY HOWITT
ILLUSTRATED BY TONY DiTERLIZZI

Picture Book

"Tony DiTerlizzi has breathed life (and, alas, death!) into a creepy, classic poem by penning macabre, intricately detailed black-and-white drawings on silvery pages, creating the perfect backdrop for a spider's Victorian dwellings and a damselfly's flapper-inspired outfits. This book will undoubtedly spin a silky web around you at Halloween, or any other time of year!"

—**Alison Morris**, *Wellesley Booksmith*, Wellesley, MA

TOO MANY PUMPKINS

BY LINDA WHITE
ILLUSTRATED BY MEGAN LLOYD

Picture Book

"My favorite handsell at Halloween for young and old alike is *Too Many Pumpkins*. It has a wonderful message about the value of being generous and open-minded."

—**Shannon Lowry**, *The Bookery*,
Ephrata, WA

HANUKKAH

A CONFUSED HANUKKAH
AN ORIGINAL STORY OF CHELM
BY JON KOONS
ILLUSTRATED BY S.D. SCHINDLER

Picture Book

"The people in the village of Chelm have forgotten how to celebrate Hanukkah and their rabbi is away on a journey. They send Yossel to a nearby village to find out what must be done. When Yossel makes a wrong turn and ends up in a big city celebrating Christmas, the resulting celebration at Chelm is a hilarious combination of Jewish and Christian customs."

—**Beth Hull**, *The Avid Reader*, Davis, CA

HANUKKAH
A COUNTING BOOK IN ENGLISH, HEBREW, AND YIDDISH
BY EMILY SPER

Picture Book

"Striking graphics and interesting text make this a book to return to night after night. Each spread features brightly colored, die-cut candles and explanations of the symbols of Hanukkah with important words written in English, Hebrew, and Yiddish."

—**Sara Yu**, *Bank Street Bookstore*, New York, NY

CHRISTMAS

CHRISTMAS FOR A KITTEN

BY ROBIN PULVER
ILLUSTRATED BY LAYNE JOHNSON

Picture Book

"Vivid details, a complex, yet gentle tale that mixes holiday fantasy with real life, and beautiful pastel illustrations make this a great Christmas book."

—**Pat Kutz**, *Lift Bridge Book Shop,*
Brockport, NY

A CHRISTMAS LIKE HELEN'S

BY NATALIE KINSEY-WARNOCK
ILLUSTRATED BY MARY AZARIAN

Picture Book

"Natalie Kinsey-Warnock provides a recipe for an old-fashioned Vermont Christmas in this book, based on her grandmother's childhood. This warmhearted story is beautifully illustrated with woodcuts by Mary Azarian and invokes the spirit of the simple, homey joys of life at Christmastime and all year long."

—**Sandy Johnson**, *The Galaxy Bookshop,* Hardwick, VT

THE CHRISTMAS SHIP
BY DEAN MORRISSEY

Picture Book

"With the help of animated toys, two children board a magical ship to help Father Christmas on Christmas Eve. Destined to be a classic Christmas tale!"

—**Emery Pinter**, *Chapter 11*,
Lawrenceville, GA

GUESS WHO'S COMING TO SANTA'S FOR DINNER?
BY TOMIE DePAOLA

Picture Book

"Tomie dePaola's latest Christmas book offers a funny look at how members of the same family can be so different—and the Claus family is no exception. Children will chuckle as the Christmas dinner starts out with some crazy mashed potatoes and ends with a bang of fiery, flaming pudding!"

—**Jessilynn Krebs**, *McLean & Eakin Booksellers*,
Petoskey, MI

THE LAST HOLIDAY CONCERT

BY ANDREW CLEMENTS

Middle Grade

"Hart Evans was always the most popular kid in elementary school, and now that he's begun middle school, everything is going his way. But when an angry choir director tells the kids that they will have to plan their own concert, everyone learns some valuable lessons. As for the holiday concert, well, just make sure you have tissues on hand when you read the end because I guarantee you will cry."

—Sara Chaganti, *The Bookloft,* Enterprise, OR

AN ORANGE FOR FRANKIE

BY PATRICIA POLACCO

Picture Book

"Once again, Patricia Polacco shares a family story that poignantly brings home the importance of strong values and family traditions, which are too often forgotten. Sure to become a holiday favorite!"

—Marilynn Bernhard, *Chesterfield Books,*
Chesterfield Township, MI

GENERAL

THE KIDS' HOLIDAY BAKING BOOK
150 FAVORITE DESSERT RECIPES FROM AROUND THE WORLD
❧ BY ROSEMARY BLACK

All Ages

"What a great collection of recipes. Breaking it down by holiday and including so many multicultural suggestions makes it a title we are likely to sell many of this holiday season. Good work!"

—**Gayle Shanks**, *Changing Hands Bookstore*, Tempe, AZ

MORE TO CELEBRATE

In the United States, we're lucky to have a diverse population, which means we get to celebrate a lot of holidays! Here are some additional picture books for kids.

—**Sara Yu,** *Bank Street Bookstore*, New York, NY

Chinese New Year

Happy, Happy Chinese New Year!, by Demi

Lion Dancer: Ernie Wan's Chinese New Year, by Kate Waters and Madeline Slovenz-Low, illustrated (photographs) by Martha Cooper

My First Chinese New Year, by Karen Katz

Day of the Dead

Day of the Dead, by Tony Johnston, illustrated by Jeanette
  Winter

Diwali

Lighting a Lamp: A Diwali Story, by Jonny Zucker, illustrated
  by Jan Barger

The Story of Divaali, retold by Jatinder Verma,
  illustrated by Nilesh Mistry

Kwanzaa

K Is for Kwanzaa, by Juwanda G. Ford,
  illustrated by Ken Wilson-Max

A Kwanzaa Celebration Pop-Up Book,
  by Nancy Williams, illustrated by Robert Sabuda

My First Kwanzaa, by Karen Katz

Ramadan

Celebrating Ramadan, by Diane Hoyt-Goldsmith,
  illustrated (photographs) by Lawrence Migdale

Fasting and Dates: A Ramadan and Eid-ul-Fitr Story,
  by Jonny Zucker, illustrated by Jan Barger

Ramadan, by Suhaib Hamid Ghazi,
  illustrated by Omar Rayyan

Three Kings Day

Three Kings Day, by Diane Hoyt-Goldsmith,
  illustrated (photographs) by Lawrence Migdale

❧ WHAT TO READ WHILE YOU'RE WAITING FOR THE NEXT HARRY POTTER

CHECK OUT THESE OTHER GREAT READS RECOMMENDED by independent booksellers from across the USA. These books are sure to please readers of all ages.

1. *Eragon*, by Christopher Paolini

2. *Children of the Lamp: The Akhenaten Adventure*, by Philip Kerr
   First volume in the Akhenaten Adventure series

3. *Inkheart*, by Cornelia Funke

4. *Septimus Heap, Book One: Magyk*, by Angie Sage, Mark Zug (Illus.)
   First volume in the Septimus Heap series

5. *Dragon Rider*, by Cornelia Funke

6. *The Amulet of Samarkand*, by Jonathan Stroud
   First volume in the Bartimaeus Trilogy

7. *Midnight for Charlie Bone*, by Jenny Nimmo
   First volume in the Children of the Red King series

8. *The Field Guide*, by Tony DiTerlizzi and Holly Black
   First volume in the The Spiderwick Chronicles

9. *The Saint of Dragons*, by Jason Hightman

10. *Artemis Fowl*, by Eoin Colfer
    First volume in the Artemis Fowl series

11. *Beyond the Deepwoods*, by Paul Stewart
    and Chris Riddell
    First volume in the Edge Chronicles

12. *The Sea of Trolls*, by Nancy Farmer

13. *The Thief Lord*, by Cornelia Funke

14. *Gregor the Overlander*, by Suzanne Collins
    First volume in the Underland Chronicles series

15. *Lionboy*, by Zizou Corder
    First volume in the Lionboy trilogy

16. *The Fellowship of the Ring*, by J.R.R. Tolkien
    First volume in the Lord of the Rings series

17. *Peter and the Starcatchers*, by Dave Barry
    and Ridley Pearson

18. *So You Want to Be a Wizard*, by Diane Duane
    First volume in the Young Wizards series

19. *The Magician's Nephew*, by C.S. Lewis
    First volume in the The Chronicles of Narnia series

20. *The Valley of Secrets*, by Charmian Hussey

❧ FAVORITE SERIES

AGES 6 – 8

The Absent Author (A to Z Mysteries), by Ron Roy, illustrated, by John Steven Gurney

Amber Brown, by Paula Danziger

Arthur, by Marc Brown

Geronimo Stilton, by Geronimo Stilton

Hank the Cowdog, by John R. Erickson, illustrated by Gerald L. Holmes

Jenny Archer, by Ellen Conford

Junie B. Jones, by Barbara Park, illustrated by Denise Brunkus

Magic Tree House, by Mary Pope Osborne, illustrated by Sal Murdocca

Secrets of Droon, by Tony Abbott

Spiderwick Chronicles, by Tony DiTerlizzi and Holly Black

Walter the Farting Dog, by William Kotzwinkle and Glenn Murray, illustrated by Audrey Colman

MIDDLE GRADE

The Adventures of Tintin, by Hergé

Alex Rider Adventures, by Anthony Horowitz

Anastasia, by Lois Lowry

Artemis Fowl, by Eoin Colfer

Charlie Bone (Children of the Red King), by Jenny Nimmo

Cirque du Freak, by Darren Shan

MIDDLE GRADE *(continued)*

The Curse of the Blue Figurine (A John Bellairs Mystery Featuring Johnny Dixon), by John Bellairs

The Dark Is Rising, by Susan Cooper

The Prydain Chronicles, by Lloyd Alexander

Redwall, by Brian Jacques

A Series of Unfortunate Events, by Lemony Snicket

A Wrinkle in Time, by Madeleine L'Engle

YOUNG ADULT

Abarat, by Clive Barker

The Abhorsen Trilogy, by Garth Nix

Arthur Trilogy, by Kevin Crossley-Holland

The Clique, by Lisi Harrison

Confessions of Georgia Nicolson, by Louise Rennison

Discworld, by Terry Pratchett

The Earthsea Cycle, by Ursula K. Le Guin

Gossip Girl, by Cecily Vin Ziegesar

The Princess Diaries, by Meg Cabot

The Sisterhood of the Traveling Pants, by Ann Brashares

❧ BOOKSTORE FAVORITES ON THE BIG SCREEN

Over the years, many popular family films have been inspired by children's books, driving young readers to seek out the original stories. This is a list of great reads (by no means exhaustive) that have become recent box-office hits and timeless classics.

Alice in Wonderland, by Lewis Carroll

Around the World in Eighty Days, by Jules Verne

The Bear, by James Oliver Curwood

Because of Winn-Dixie, by Kate DiCamillo

Black Beauty, by Anna Sewell

The Black Stallion, by Walter Farley

The Borrowers, by Mary Norton

The Cat in the Hat, by Dr. Seuss

Charlie and the Chocolate Factory, by Roald Dahl

Cheaper by the Dozen, by Frank B. Gilbreth, Jr., and Ernestine Gilbreth Carey

The Chronicles of Narnia, by C. S. Lewis

Confessions of a Teenage Drama Queen, by Dyan Sheldon

Curious George, by H. A. Rey

The Story of Dr. Dolittle, by Hugh Lofting

Ella Enchanted, by Gail Carson Levine

Freaky Friday, by Mary Rodgers

Harry Potter series, by J. K. Rowling

Holes, by Louis Sachar

How the Grinch Stole Christmas, by Dr. Seuss

Jumanji, by Chris Van Allsburg

A Little Princess, by Frances Hodgson Burnett

Little Women, by Louisa May Alcott

The Lord of the Rings, by J. R. R. Tolkien

Mary Poppins, by P. L. Travers

Matilda, by Roald Dahl

The Neverending Story, by Michael Ende

Oliver Twist, by Charles Dickens

The Outsiders, by S. E. Hinton

Peter Pan, by J. M. Barrie

The Polar Express, by Chris Van Allsburg

The Princess Diaries, by Meg Cabot

A Series of Unfortunate Events, by Lemony Snicket

The Secret Garden, by Frances Hodgson Burnett

Shrek!, by William Steig

The Sisterhood of the Traveling Pants, by Ann Brashares

Stuart Little, by E. B. White

Tuck Everlasting, by Natalie Babbitt

Whale Rider, by Witi Ihimaera

Winnie-the-Pooh, by A. A. Milne

The Wizard of Oz, by L. Frank Baum

Zathura, by Chris Van Allsburg

Alice the Fairy cover illustration, copyright © 2004 by David Shannon

Index

ABOUT THE CONTRIBUTORS

BOOK SENSE
A wholly owned subsidiary of the American Booksellers Association, Book Sense, Inc., founded in 1999, administers the Book Sense integrated marketing and branding campaign. Book Sense, comprised of 1,200 bookstore locations in 50 states, seeks to build a national identity for independent bookstores while celebrating the unique character of each store; to create awareness of independent booksellers across the country; and to underscore the collective strength of independent booksellers to consumers. Book Sense includes the Book Sense Picks, the Book Sense Bestseller Lists, a national gift card program, and BookSense.com. *Book Sense Best Books* was the first book published under its auspices.

THE AMERICAN BOOKSELLERS ASSOCIATION (ABA) Founded in 1900, the American Booksellers Association (www.bookweb.org) is a not-for-profit trade organization devoted to meeting the needs of its core members—independently owned bookstores with retail storefront locations—through advocacy, education, research, and information dissemination.

MARK NICHOLS was an independent bookseller in various locations from Maine to Connecticut from 1976 through 1993. After seven years in a variety of positions with major publishers, he joined the ABA in 2000, and currently serves as the Director of Book Sense Marketing. He is the editor of *Book Sense Best Books* and *Book Sense Best Children's Books*.

CORNELIA FUNKE has become one of today's most beloved writers of magical stories for children of all ages. Her best-selling books include *The Thief Lord*, *Inkheart*, *Dragon Rider*, *The Princess Knight*, and *Inkspell* (a sequel to *Inkheart*). A Book Sense Book of the Year award winner for children's literature, she lives in Hamburg, Germany, with her husband and children.

About the Illustrators

JANE DYER is the beloved illustrator of many books, including *When Mama Comes Home Tonight*, by Eileen Spinnelli, and *New York Times* bestsellers *Time for Bed*, by Mem Fox, and *I Love You Like Crazy Cakes*, by Rose Lewis. Her writing credits include the *Little Brown Bear* series and *Animal Crackers*. She lives with her husband in Northampton, Massachusetts, and they spend summers in Cummington, Massachusetts.

IAN FALCONER, when he's not working on *Olivia*, spends his time designing sets and costumes for the New York City Ballet, the San Francisco Opera, and the Royal Opera House in London and creating memorable covers for the *New Yorker*. A Book Sense Book of the Year award winner for children's literature, Falconer lives in New York City.

BRETT HELQUIST grew up in Utah and Arizona with his six sisters. As kids, they didn't visit many museums. He says his love of art came from all the comic books he read. Brett is the illustrator of the *New York Times* bestselling *Series of Unfortunate Events*, by Lemony Snicket, the award-winning *Chasing Vermeer*, and the picture book *Milly and the Macy's Parade*, by Shana Corey. A Book Sense Book of the

Year award winner for children's literature, he lives in Brooklyn, New York, with his wife.

BETSY LEWIN is the Caldecott Honor-winning illustrator of *Click, Clack, Moo: Cows That Type* and its *New York Times* bestselling sequels *Giggle, Giggle, Quack* and *Duck for President*. A Book Sense Book of the Year award winner for children's literature, her other picture books include *Click, Clack Quackity-Quack*; *Two Eggs Please*; and *So, What's It Like to Be a Cat?* She lives in Brooklyn, New York.

JON J MUTH's picture books, including *Zen Shorts, Gershon's Monster,* and *Stone Soup,* have met with widespread acclaim and are embraced by readers of all ages. His many awards and honors include a Gold Medal from the Society of Illustrators for *Come On, Rain!,* by Karen Hesse. His own story, *The Three Questions,* which was based on a short story by Leo Tolstoy, was described by the *New York Times Book Review* as "quietly life-changing."

DAVID SHANNON, born in Washington, DC, grew up in Spokane, Washington. After graduating from art school in Pasadena, California, he lived in New York City until 1992. His editorial illustrations have appeared in the *New York Times*, *Time*, and *Rolling Stone*, and his artwork has adorned numerous book jackets. His books include *Duck on a Bike*; *No, David!*; and *Alice the Fairy*. Shannon now lives in Burbank, California, with his wife, Heidi and his daughter, Emma.

PETER SÍS is an internationally acclaimed illustrator, author, and filmmaker from Czechoslovakia. He became one of the leading artists in the field with the publication of the 1987 Newbery Medal Winner, *The Whipping Boy*, by Sid Fleishman. Sís has more than twenty books to his credit, including *The New York Times Book Review* Best Illustrated Book of the Year winners *Rainbow Rhino*, *Follow the Dream*, *Komodo!*, *Beach Ball*, and *The Three Golden Keys*, as well as *The Train of States*, *The Tree of Life*, and *Madlenka*. Sís lives in the New York City area with his wife, daughter, and son.

MARK TEAGUE has been tickling the funny bones and imaginations of kids for more than fifteen years, illustrating the *Poppleton* series by Cynthia Rylant and his own *Detective LaRue* series. His book, *How Do Dinosaurs Say Good Night?*, written by Jane Yolen, was named an ALA Notable Book and a Book Sense Book of the Year Finalist. A Book Sense Book of the Year award winner for children's literature, Mark lives in Coxsackie, New York, with his wife and their two young daughters.

About the Booksellers

ELLEN DAVIS, President of the Association of Booksellers for Children, is the owner of Dragonwings, a favorite destination for local and vacationing families and one of four independent bookstores in the small midwestern town of Waupaca, Wisconsin. She lives with her family in a rambling, country home, and when she isn't reading, she loves gardening, baking, silent sports, and hosting myriad celebrations.

RENÉ KIRKPATRICK has been a bookseller for 27 years, and is currently with All for Kids Books & Music, Seattle's premiere independent family-owned children's bookstore. She and her husband live in Seattle, Washington, surrounded by books, music, and pets.

VALERIE KOEHLER is a reader, wife, mom, daughter, sister, and owner of Blue Willow Bookshop in Houston, Texas, in no particular order. She grew up reading under the nursery nightlight, later by the early morning sun in the car pool line, and now on the couch with her reading glasses. Valerie says, "Life is a journey that we share with the world through books."

JOSIE LEAVITT and ELIZABETH BLUEMLE have been children's booksellers since they opened Flying Pig Children's Books in 1996 in Charlotte, Vermont. Before opening the bookstore, Josie was a stand-up comic in New York City. Elizabeth was a teacher and school librarian, and is the author of two picture books forthcoming from Candlewick Press.

ALISON MORRIS is the children's book buyer for Wellesley Booksmith, a kid-friendly independent bookstore in Wellesley, Massachusetts. She is currently writing a nonfiction children's book that features quirky tales from women's history.

JUDY NELSON, her husband of 37 years, Byron, and two of their four children, Laura and Pat, work together in their growing book business. She opened Mrs. Nelson's Toy and Book Shop in Laverne, California, in 1985 and has since opened two branches of Mrs. Nelson's Book Fair Company. She also began Mrs. Nelson's Book Company this year, a business that sells books to school libraries.

DINAH PAUL was raised in Louisville, Kentucky, in a family of six where she first discovered the magic of the written word. After receiving a bachelors degree in English, she fulfilled a life-long dream of owning a children's bookstore. Dinah now spends her days in Alexandria, Virginia, with her husband, Josh, and her puppy, Finnegan, as the proud owner of A Likely Story Children's Bookstore.

BETH PUFFER became a bookseller 32 years ago and has spent the past 19 years with Bank Street Bookstore in New York City. A stint as a sales rep gave her an invaluable look at the other side of the publishing business, but also confirmed which side of the counter she truly belongs behind. Despite the long hours and all the challenges of bookselling, she can think of no better career than one that allows her to order books, unpack them, and hand-sell each one to a happy customer.

SARA YU is the assistant manager of Bank Street Bookstore and has been a children's bookseller for eight years. She lives in New York City with her boyfriend and a very big dog.

ACKNOWLEDGMENTS

FOREMOST, THANKS MUST GO TO THOSE INDEPENDENT booksellers with Book Sense whose recommendations form the core of this volume. We are very appreciative of the dedication and enthusiasm with which they approach their craft and their willingness to share their knowledge and experience both in their stores and throughout these pages. Special thanks to those booksellers whose essays appear as introductions to each section, and to Beth Puffer and Sara Yu of Bank Street Bookstore for their keen eyes and expertise.

Gratitude to Esther Margolis, Heidi Sachner, Shannon Berning, Keith Hollaman, Anna Szymanski, Harry Burton, Kevin McGuinness, Paul Sugarman, and the entire staff of Newmarket Press for their energy, creativity, kindness, and true caring demonstrated along every step of this project, and to Newmarket's trade distributor, W. W. Norton, for their special attention and support. Once again, working with two distinguished independent publishers has proven to be a most rewarding experience.

Thanks also to those many other publishers, large and small, for their continued support of the Book Sense program. Special thanks to FSG, HarperCollins, Scholastic, and Simon & Schuster for their assistance in procuring illustrations for this volume, and to Jane Dyer, Ian Falconer, Brett Helquist, Betsy Lewin, Jon J Muth, David Shannon, Peter Sis, and Mark Teague for giving permission to reproduce their wonderful artwork.

Finally to the staff of the American Booksellers Association, past and present, whose devotion to the promotion of independent bookselling is inexhaustible. This book is further testimony to their commitment and no small reflection of their achievement.

Book Sense Books from Newmarket Press

BOOK SENSE BEST BOOKS: 125 FAVORITE BOOKS RECOMMENDED BY INDEPENDENT BOOKSELLERS
A compilation of must-read adult and children's titles recommended by trusted and experienced booksellers from across the country. This quick-and-easy reference features The Top Picks (15 adult and 10 children's titles), Top Reading Group Recommendations (50 titles, selected by theme), Top Classics for Children, and more.
112 pages 5½ x 8½ 1-55704-643-3 $12.95

BOOK SENSE BEST CHILDREN'S BOOKS: 240 FAVORITES FOR ALL AGES RECOMMENDED BY INDEPENDENT BOOKSELLERS
In this ultimate guide for parents, Book Sense booksellers from across the country offer their recommendations on more than 240 children's books for every age group: Babies and Toddlers, Picture Books for Younger Children, Picture Books for Older Children, Chapter Books, Middle Grade, Young Adult, Nonfiction, Holiday Books.

With a foreword by Cornelia Funke and illustrations from award-winning illustrators Jane Dyer, Ian Falconer, Brett Helquist, Betsy Lewin, Jon J Muth, David Shannon, Peter Sís, and Mark Teague, this is a must-have resource for parents and librarians.
176 pages 5½ x 8½ 1-55704-679-4 $14.95
